NAPOLÉON
BONAPARTE

Other Titles in the
People Who Made History Series

PEOPLE
WHO MADE
HISTORY

NAPOLÉON
BONAPARTE

Raymond and Loretta Obstfeld, *Book Editor*

Bonnie Szumski, *Editorial Director*
Stuart B. Miller, *Managing Editor*
David M. Haugen, *Series Editor*

Greenhaven Press, Inc., San Diego, CA

Every effort has been made to trace the owners of copyrighted material. The articles in this volume may have been edited for content, length, and/or reading level. The titles have been changed to enhance the editorial purpose. Those interested in locating the original source will find the complete citation on the first page of each article.

Library of Congress Cataloging-in-Publication Data

Napoléon Bonaparte / Raymond Obstfeld and Loretta Obstfeld, book editors.
     p.   cm. — (People who made history)
    Includes bibliographical references and index.
    ISBN 0-7377-0422-5 (pbk. : alk. paper) —
ISBN 0-7377-0423-3 (lib. bdg. : alk. paper)
    1. Napoléon I, Emperor of the French 1769–1821—
Influence. 2. Emperors—France—Biography. I. Obstfeld, Raymond, 1952–   II. Obstfeld, Loretta. III. Series.

DC203.N2095   2001
944.05'092—dc21   00-058689
[B]   CIP

Cover photo: © Giraudon/Art Resource, NY
Library of Congress, 16, 134
North Wind, 38, 59, 120, 150, 158
Prints Old and Rare, 173

Copyright © 2001 by Greenhaven Press, Inc.
PO Box 289009
San Diego, CA 92198-9009
Printed in the U.S.A.

Contents

Chapter 1: The Major Influences on Napoléon's Character and Career

Napoléon's relationships with his parents and brother, as well as his Corsican heritage, had a profound influence on him. He was raised by a stern, social-climbing mother, whom he held in awe, and by an ambitious, opportunistic father, whom he held in contempt. Being brought up in this volatile mixture of family and in a country in armed rebellion against France, he learned the ruthlessness and self-sufficiency he needed to achieve his dreams of power.

Although the French Revolution began in 1789 when Napoléon was only twenty years old, the unprecedented changes it brought about made his rapid advancement in the military possible. It also created in the French people a romantic desire for a strong hero to lead them, a role that Napoléon was willing to assume. Once in power, many of his most famous political accomplishments, including the Civil Code and educational reform, were the direct result of the blueprint provided by the French Revolution.

Chapter 2: Napoléon's Domestic Policies

One of Napoléon's greatest achievements was the establishment of the Civil Code, which unified all of France under one set of laws. As France's influence spread, so did the Civil Code, which is still the basis for the laws in many European countries.

Napoléon implemented an educational system in France that standardized not only what subjects were taught but also how they were taught. Although this system was extremely rigid, it gave students the opportunity to advance based on their merit and not just because of their family connections. These reforms are credited with making France a leader in science and other studies in Europe.

Chapter 3: Napoléon's Foreign Policies

and clothe his army and facing a brutal winter, Napoléon lost nearly half a million French troops, as well as his reputation for military invincibility.

Chapter 5: Napoléon's Legend and Legacy

Foreword

In the vast and colorful pageant of human history, a handful of individuals stand out. They are the men and women who have come variously to be called "great," "leading," "brilliant," "pivotal," or "infamous" because they and their deeds forever changed their own society or the world as a whole. Some were political or military leaders—kings, queens, presidents, generals, and the like—whose policies, conquests, or innovations reshaped the maps and futures of countries and entire continents. Among those falling into this category were the formidable Roman statesman/general Julius Caesar, who extended Rome's power into Gaul (what is now France); Caesar's lover and ally, the notorious Egyptian queen Cleopatra, who challenged the strongest male rulers of her day; and England's stalwart Queen Elizabeth I, whose defeat of the mighty Spanish Armada saved England from subjugation.

Some of history's other movers and shakers were scientists or other thinkers whose ideas and discoveries altered the way people conduct their everyday lives or view themselves and their place in nature. The electric light and other remarkable inventions of Thomas Edison, for example, revolutionized almost every aspect of home-life and the workplace; and the theories of naturalist Charles Darwin lit the way for biologists and other scientists in their ongoing efforts to understand the origins of living things, including human beings.

Still other people who made history were religious leaders and social reformers. The struggles of the Arabic prophet Muhammad more than a thousand years ago led to the establishment of one of the world's great religions—Islam; and the efforts and personal sacrifices of an American reverend named Martin Luther King Jr. brought about major improvements in race relations and the justice system in the United States.

Each anthology in the People Who Made History series begins with an introductory essay that provides a general overview of the individual's life, times, and contributions. The group of essays that follow are chosen for their accessibility to a young adult audience and carefully edited in consideration of the reading and comprehension levels of that audience. Some of the essays are by noted historians, professors, and other experts. Others are excerpts from contemporary writings by or about the pivotal individual in question. To aid the reader in choosing the material of immediate interest or need, an annotated table of contents summarizes the article's main themes and insights.

Each volume also contains extensive research tools, including a collection of excerpts from primary source documents pertaining to the individual under discussion. The volumes are rounded out with an extensive bibliography and a comprehensive index.

Plutarch, the renowned first-century Greek biographer and moralist, crystallized the idea behind Greenhaven's People Who Made History when he said, "To be ignorant of the lives of the most celebrated men of past ages is to continue in a state of childhood all our days." Indeed, since it is people who make history, every modern nation, organization, institution, invention, artifact, and idea is the result of the diligent efforts of one or more individuals, living or dead; and it is therefore impossible to understand how the world we live in came to be without examining the contributions of these individuals.

NAPOLÉON BONAPARTE: THE MAN WHO WOULD BE KING

Since Napoléon Bonaparte's death in 1821, he has been the subject of over two hundred thousand books. According to one historian, "Probably more has been written about him than any other historical personage except Jesus of Nazareth."[1] Perhaps the reason Napoléon has been placed in such esteemed company is because the comparison is one Napoléon himself encouraged. According to historian J. Christopher Herold, "[Napoléon's] comparison of himself with Christ seems exceptionally inappropriate; and yet . . . it was accepted without shock within a few years of his death. The myth of his martyrdom was only part of the mythology manufactured at St. Helena, thanks to which he became the deified son of the common people."[2] The difference, of course, is that while Jesus focused his attention on the spiritual world, Napoléon's sights were clearly aimed at the material world. And while Jesus persuaded with words and ideas, Napoléon conquered with muskets and cannons.

FAMILY HISTORY

One of the great ironies of Napoléon's life was that he ruled and was adored by a people he had vehemently hated as a child. Napoléone Buonaparte—the spelling he used until 1795—was born August 15, 1769, in Ajaccio, the capital of the island of Corsica, only fifteen months after France had acquired Corsica from Italy. His father had fought against the French on the side of the Corsican resistance leader Pasquale Paoli. Legend has it that Napoléon was born in a cave while his parents hid from French soldiers trying to put down a local rebellion.

Though the Buonapartes were not wealthy, neither were they poor. Napoléon's father, Charles Buonaparte, and mother, Maria Laetizia Ramolino, struggled over money matters for most of their turbulent marriage. Some of their

11

money woes were caused by the need to provide for eight children. Napoléon was their fourth child, but only the second to survive.

Charles Buonaparte spent most of his time trying to support his family by seeking jobs from the new French governor. Finally, in 1779, Charles secured the position of deputy for the nobility of Corsica at the court of Louis XVI. He took his two oldest sons, Joseph and Napoléon, and moved to France, leaving his wife in Corsica to care for the other children.

NAPOLÉON'S EDUCATION

While Joseph was supposedly destined to become a Roman Catholic priest, Napoléon seemed destined for a military career and was awarded a scholarship to the military school of Brienne. He was ten years old. Napoléon's stay at Brienne was a painful experience. Ceaselessly teased for his short, skinny body and poor French—Napoléon had been raised speaking Italian—he proved to be a mediocre student in most subjects, though he had a passion for history and geography. He particularly studied Julius Caesar, whom Napoléon considered to embody the virtues of being a warrior, statesman, and writer. It would not be long before Napoléon, too, would embody all of those traits, although it is for history to decide if in his hands these were virtues or vices.

Though Napoléon was only fourteen when he left Brienne in 1784, he managed to make a few friends there, who later were rewarded for their loyalty. One classmate eventually would be appointed his councilor of state, another would be named prefect of the Marne, and his school principal would be promoted to headmaster of the more prestigious lycée, or high school, of Reims.

Upon leaving Brienne, Napoléon entered the Paris military school of the Champ-de-Mars. There, he acquitted himself much better as a student. He excelled in mathematics, which resulted in his appointment as lieutenant of artillery after completing only one year of study, when two years were normally required for such an appointment.

EARLY MILITARY CAREER

After graduation Napoléon was immediately assigned to the Regiment de la Fère of the Royal Corps of Artillery, stationed at Valence, where he studied military theories and infantry maneuvers. His days were mostly uneventful, even boring, and the young Corsican did not find military life very engaging. In fact, between 1785 and 1791 he took over three years of leave, more time than he spent in actual duty. In his spare time he devoured many literary works, including those of French philosopher Jean-Jacques Rousseau, who was a champion of Corsican independence, a topic close to Napoléon's heart. True to that cause, he spent much of his three years of leave back in Corsica, working for its independence from France, even though he was a French military officer. He even helped form a national citizen guard, contrary to the orders of the French authorities.

Then, in 1789, Corsica was officially incorporated into France, and Corsicans were given full rights as French citizens. Napoléon, along with most Corsicans, considered this a courageous and generous act on the part of the French government and the independence movement died out. From this time on, Napoléon began to see himself more as a Frenchman and less as a Corsican.

THE FRENCH REVOLUTION

Napoléon's relatively humble origins, coupled with his lackluster dedication as a soldier, did not bode well for his military career. But the political turmoil caused by the French Revolution in 1789 provided opportunities for him that ordinarily would not have been available to someone of his class. The French Revolution, as with the American Revolution that helped inspire it, was due in large part to a desire of the middle class for a more democratic rule. At the time of the Revolution, France was the wealthiest and most populous nation in Europe, with 25 million people compared to Great Britain's 9 million or Prussia's 8.6 million. Paris was the largest city in Europe and its populace the best educated. Yet France was divided into three very distinct social classes, called *états*, or estates. The upper class, known as the First Estate, comprised 130,000 members of the clergy; the Second Estate consisted of the 400,000 members of the nobility; the remaining 24 million, mostly peasants, workers, and tradespeople, were known as the Third Estate. With the First and Second Estates controlling most of the wealth and enjoying freedoms denied everyone else, eventually France erupted into revolution.

The rebels' first steps were to abolish the privileges granted to the French aristocracy and the clergy. Next, a constitutional government was established and the monarchy's power was radically limited. The revolutionaries were not necessarily opposed to a France being led by a monarch, but they preferred one chosen by a representative government rather than a king or queen who was merely born into the job. In addition, supporters of the French Revolution wanted to bring about a society in which advancement was by merit rather than by class privilege. It was this principle of civil equality that paved the way for Napoléon's own advancement.

ALLEGIANCE TO CORSICA

By 1792, twenty-one-year-old Napoléon had been promoted to the rank of first lieutenant. That year, in keeping with his revolutionary fervor, Napoléon requested and was granted a transfer from the regular army to a volunteer Corsican battalion that was fighting opponents of the Revolution. When the regular army issued orders for all officers to rejoin their regiments, Napoléon refused to return in order to continue fighting in Corsica.

Napoléon let nothing stand in his way as he fought the Revolution's enemies. In the streets of Ajaccio, Corsica's capital, he demonstrated some of his characteristic ruthlessness against "the rabble" by opening fire on protesters, kidnapping opponents, and disobeying his commander's orders by capturing the citadel. Napoléon's violent methods so outraged his opponents that he was denounced to the Legislative Assembly and to Corsican political leaders in Paris.

Napoléon then demonstrated his other dominant characteristic: political savvy. Realizing that his position in Corsica was now shaky, he hurried back to Paris to be reinstated in the regular army. Once reinstated, however, he again returned to Corsica—using the excuse that he had to accompany his younger sister home after her convent was disbanded. Upon arrival in Corsica, he rejoined his old battalion at the rank of lieutenant colonel.

In 1792 France's revolutionary government, flush with popularity at home and believing that the common people of other countries were waiting to be liberated by them, decided the time was right to declare war on Austria and Prussia. During this war the French government decided to use Corsica as a base from which to invade the neighboring island kingdom of Sardinia, which was allied with Austria. Napoléon's Corsican battalion was sent on a subsidiary invasion of yet another island, Maddalena. Napoléon acquitted himself well, commanding an artillery assault that nearly brought the island's fort to surrender.

Napoléon's allegiance to Corsica was about to come to an unexpected end, however. When Paoli, who had in the past led Corsica's independence movement, again broke with France, he was arrested as a traitor and an agent of England, which had just joined Austria and Prussia against France. His arrest was, in part, the result of a heated denunciation by Napoléon's younger brother Lucien, a strong supporter of French rule. The town of Ajaccio erupted in protest. The Buonapartes were now the objects of hatred from both opposing factions—those who had supported Paoli and those who had backed Carlo Pozzo di Borgo, a Corsican diplomat who opposed Napoléon in Corsican politics. The mobs ransacked the Buonaparte home, forcing Napoléon's mother and sisters to flee Corsica for France. From this point on Napoléon was loyal to the French side in all matters relating to Corsica.

HIS MILITARY CAREER IS RESUMED

With Corsica now behind him, twenty-four-year-old Napoléon was given command of an artillery company in his old regiment. On September 16, 1793, his long-awaited opportunity to distinguish himself in battle finally came. The important French shipping city of Toulon had been captured by the British, and the French army was attempting to reclaim the city. When the commanding officer of the artillery was wounded, Napoléon was sent in to replace him. Once again Napoléon demonstrated a shrewd combination of military strategy—necessary to win battles—and political awareness— necessary to promote that win into career advancement. Napoléon believed Toulon could be retaken by an artillery attack on the fort of Eguillette, which controlled the city's harbor. But the attack had to be launched immediately, before British reinforcements arrived. "Take Eguillette," Napoléon advised, "and you will be in Toulon in eight days."[3]

However, Napoléon's commanding officer did not follow his advice and the siege foundered. There was talk of abandoning the battle altogether and conceding the province to the British. But Napoléon was not easily dissuaded. Going over

his commander's head, he
submitted a plan of attack
to officials back in Paris. As
a result, Napoléon's reluc-
tant commander was re-
placed, the battle plan was
enacted, and Toulon was
recaptured. The French
government took notice of
this brash soldier who was
described by France's revolutionary leader Augustin
de Robespierre as an "ar-
tillery general of transcen-
dent merit."[4]

Napoléon Bonaparte

With the support of Au-
gustin de Robespierre and
his brother, Maximilien, Napoléon's rise through military
ranks was remarkably swift. A few months after the victory
at Toulon, he was appointed brigadier general and was
given command of artillery in France's Army of Italy.

For Napoléon, disaster struck on July 27, 1794. The Robes-
pierres fell out of favor, and all those whom they had cham-
pioned fell under suspicion—Napoléon included. Napoléon
was arrested and was imprisoned for trying to destroy liberty.
However, he was released ten days later, and his rank was reinstated when no reasonable charges could be proven.

Napoléon's troubles were not over. Suspicious that Corsican officers might harbor some British loyalties, the French
government transferred all Corsicans from the Army of Italy
to the much less desirable Army of the West. Napoléon refused to transfer, claiming illness. Instead, by pulling political strings, he got himself appointed head of the Topograph-
ical Bureau, where he distinguished himself by modernizing
military maps and statistics. The appointment was only a
temporary reprieve, however. Napoléon had relied on the
patronage of a member of France's Committee of Public
Safety. When his patron was removed from the committee,
Napoléon was stripped of his general's rank for refusing to
join the Army of the West.

Part of the genius of Napoléon was that he learned how to
endure misfortune while taking the greatest possible advantage of any opportunity to succeed. He once said, "Is it be-

cause [great men] are lucky that they become great? No, but being great, they have been able to master luck."[5] And so, just when it seemed that the Corsican was once again at the end of his career, he mastered his luck by taking advantage of another unexpected opportunity. French popular opinion had turned against the government after particularly bloody purges of political opponents and the passing of undemocratic laws. When a mob estimated to be near eighty thousand threatened the government building Tuileries, a mere five thousand troops were available for protection. The commander of the troops remembered Napoléon's success with artillery at Toulon and sent for him. Napoléon proved up to the task, repulsing the crowd by firing cannons point-blank into the mob. This efficient ruthlessness won him the gratitude of the nervous French government and a promotion to major general as well as an appointment as a commander of the Army of the Interior.

PERSONAL LIFE

Napoléon's roller-coaster military career was duplicated in his personal life as well. His private passions included writing and women, but in neither arena did he meet with great success. He wrote political essays, short stories, and novels; none found an appreciative audience.

Napoléon's first great romance was with his sister-in-law Désirée Clary. She was the daughter of a merchant from Marseilles, and her sister was married to Napoléon's older brother, Joseph. Though he and Clary were to be married, Napoléon seemed to lose interest in the relationship with his rapid rise to power. Napoléon, caught up in his new importance as commander of the Army of the Interior, and in the social life in Paris, soon proposed marriage to Madame Permon, a longtime friend of his father, but she laughingly dismissed his proposal by reminding him that she was old enough to be his mother.

Eventually Napoléon met Joséphine de Beauharnais, a thirty-three-year-old widow seven years his senior. She came from a wealthy, aristocratic family, but the French Revolution had left her poor; her husband had been guillotined during the Revolution. "I was certainly not insensible to feminine charms, but I had never till then been spoilt by women," Napoléon said, recounting their first meeting. "My character rendered me naturally timid in their company. Madame de

Beauharnais was the first woman who gave me any degree of confidence."[6] Historians agree that his love for her was genuine and that he relentlessly courted her until they were married in 1796. Napoléon and his new wife had little time together before he had to return to duty, this time as commander of France's Army of Italy. He was twenty-six years old.

NAPOLÉON CONQUERS ITALY

Once in Italy, Napoléon lost no time in fulfilling the potential he had shown earlier as both a remarkable military strategist and a daring politician. Within ten days of his arrival in Italy, he had achieved four major victories and established a fast-striking, highly mobile style of combat, which, even two hundred years later, is still used by many military leaders. While most generals would have been content to rest on the laurels of their military victories, Napoléon used these successes to gather more political power. He signed an armistice with Italy, although he lacked the authority to do so. However, France's leaders, known as the Directory, were pleased with the general's results—annexation of Savoy and Nice and a payment of 3 million francs—and were in no position to reprimand him for overstepping his boundaries. Napoléon demonstrated even more sophisticated political awareness when the Directory ordered him to "extinguish the flame of religious fanaticism"[7] by taking over the Vatican. Not one to underestimate the Catholic Church's influence, Napoléon instead informed the Vatican that he would not attack the pope and the church he represented—but he extracted over 15 million francs in cash and another 4 million francs' worth of art and rare books and manuscripts in return for his promise.

The Italian campaign established Napoléon's subsequent pattern of behavior. He defied or manipulated orders from his government, but he consistently won battles and then extracted enormous payments of cash and valuable material from the defeated enemies. But this strategy exposed what subsequently proved to be Napoléon's blind spot: Even though the Italians embraced the constitutional principles of the French Revolution that Napoléon brought to them, they greatly resented the French as conquerors. In future campaigns, Napoléon was to make this same mistake of ignoring the intensity of nationalism in Spain, Germany, and Russia.

The Italian campaign was important because the money

taken from the conquered Italians prevented a financial crisis in France, thereby keeping the government stable. This gave Napoléon enormous power in Paris, where the politicians realized they relied on him to maintain their own positions. Also, contrary to the self-perpetuated myth of the simple-living soldier, Napoléon pillaged his enemies in order to amass his own personal fortune. When he returned to Paris, it was as a wealthy, popular political force, someone who could make his own rules. "I no longer know how to obey,"[8] he announced upon his arrival.

THE EGYPTIAN CAMPAIGN

Although Italy had fallen, Britain and France were still at war. Napoléon's reward for his success in Italy was to be nominated as commander in chief of the Army of England and given the opportunity to plan an invasion of Britain. However, after inspecting the French navy, Napoléon realized that the superior English navy would easily defeat them before they had even landed their troops. Wisely, he advised that invasion plans be delayed. But Napoléon realized that in order to maintain his popularity and political influence, he would need to continue winning battles. "In Paris, nothing is remembered for long. If I remain doing nothing for long, I am lost."[9] So he mounted a campaign to conquer Egypt, even though that country was part of the Ottoman Empire, which had so far remained neutral in France's war with Britain. Napoléon justified the invasion by pointing out that control of Egypt would give the French more direct access to India, which they hoped to conquer.

To keep the English from realizing his intentions and sending ships to the Mediterranean, Napoléon continued to pretend that he planned to invade England. He left 30,000 soldiers camped on the northern coast of France, along with the French fleet. Meanwhile, he embarked for Egypt with 400 ships and 38,000 soldiers. Aware of the historical value of Egypt's antiquities, Napoléon included in his expedition a Commission of Arts and Sciences that consisted of over 150 scientists, engineers, and archaeologists.

Despite a number of military victories and a concentrated effort to improve living conditions for the people of Egypt, ultimately the campaign was a failure. England still controlled the Mediterranean and increased its presence in the region. The Egyptians declared a holy war against the French, and

Napoléon and his army were under constant assault. Moreover, Turkey declared war on France, as did a new alliance of England, Russia, and the Italian city-state of Naples.

A little over a year after his triumphant landing in Egypt, Napoléon was ordered to return to France. One last victory over the Turkish army before leaving helped the campaign appear victorious, despite the reality that Egypt had been a costly defeat. He entered Paris as a conquering hero, more popular than ever.

REBELLION IN THE FRENCH GOVERNMENT

Napoléon returned to a government in turmoil. The French middle class had lost faith in the Directory, which was too weak to defend the rights won in the French Revolution. The government itself was set up without a means to resolve disputes between the executive and legislative branches of government. This resulted in the ousting of elected legislators and the occasional forced removal of members of the Directory. Severe economic problems, corruption, rebellions by people still loyal to the monarchy, and the war against England and its allies all added to France's woes.

Napoléon also returned to a marriage in turmoil. In Egypt he had received reports that Joséphine had been repeatedly unfaithful, and he was determined to divorce her. Napoléon had not been a faithful husband either, however. While in Egypt he had taken as his lover the wife of one of his officers, who promptly divorced her. Napoléon's plan was to divorce Joséphine and marry his new lover. But upon seeing his wife again, Napoléon's resolve faltered and they were reconciled.

Meanwhile, several members of the Directory—Emmanuel Sieyès, Paul de Barras, and Pierre-Roger Ducos— were plotting a coup d'état that would give them control of the government. However, for this coup to succeed, they needed a strong and popular general to back them. Napoléon, though not their first choice, agreed to join them. Though ill conceived and poorly executed, nearly resulting in Napoléon's arrest or death, the coup d'état of 18–19 Brumaire (November 9–10, 1799) ended the rule of the Directory.

FROM GENERAL TO FIRST CONSUL

Those who had conspired with Napoléon had hoped to use him to further their own political ambitions. But they had not counted on the depth of Napoléon's own ambition.

Within a short time he was able to consolidate his power until he was in command of those who had given him that power in the first place.

Napoléon's first course of action that year was to write France's Constitution of the Year VIII (the years being counted from the onset of the French Revolution). Sieyès and the others who had supported Napoléon wanted a constitution that would establish a senate (called the College of Conservatives) that would in effect rule the country while Napoléon would be grand elector, the symbolic but powerless head of state. Napoléon rejected this idea, for he had no intention of settling for symbolic status when real power was within his reach. He supported a constitution that would establish three consuls as head of state. All three would be named by the senate to ten-year terms, with no limits on the number of terms one could serve. The three consuls would not be equal, however. The first consul would not be responsible to the legislature and would have law-making and law-enforcing power. In addition, he would have the power to fill important government positions. The other two consuls were merely consultants. At his insistence, Napoléon was, of course, chosen as first consul.

In 1799 a popular election was held to ratify the constitution. The reported result was 3,011,117 in favor with 1,562 opposed. However, Napoléon's brother Lucien, who was minister of the interior, had added votes to the "yes" side. In reality, Napoléon's constitution was approved by a minority of eligible voters. That did not change the practical outcome, though: Thirty-year-old Napoléon Bonaparte was now the most powerful person in France.

Napoléon immediately began to reorganize the administration of finances, justice, and police—all part of the legacy he had inherited from the French Revolution. He appointed officials carefully, first making sure of their loyalty to him. During the next two years he improved the country's woeful financial situation and stabilized its tumultuous political situation.

NEGOTIATIONS WITH THE CATHOLIC CHURCH

Although Napoléon made significant progress in reorganizing the government, he still faced opposition from royalists, who wanted the monarchy to return to rule France. And there were those, especially among the generals, who felt that Napoléon had betrayed the principles of the Revolution.

Even Napoléon's own brother Lucien—who had twice saved Napoléon's life and career—published an unflattering pamphlet entitled, "Parallel Between Caesar, Cromwell, and Bonaparte." In other words, Napoléon had no shortage of enemies—as evidenced by several assassination attempts, including a bomb that barely missed him but killed twenty-six other people.

To regain his popular appeal, Napoléon decided to offer an olive branch to the Catholic Church, which had lost most of its political influence since the French Revolution. Though he privately denied a belief in God, Napoléon recognized that such a conciliatory move would be well received by the dominantly Catholic French people. Still, Napoléon kept the church on a short leash. According to Napoléon, "The people need a religion; this religion must be in the hands of the government."[10] The agreement between Napoléon and Pope Pius VII, called the Concordat, returned some power to the church, but the church continued to be heavily monitored by the French government. As he had predicted, the French people responded enthusiastically to this overture, and Napoléon was more popular than ever. But opposition to the agreement in the legislature and military forced Napoléon to add to the Concordat—without consulting the pope—the so-called Organic Articles, which increased the French government's control over the Catholic Church. The Concordat was ratified in 1802.

DOMESTIC IMPROVEMENTS

With his power consolidated, Napoléon concentrated his public policy in two areas: education and law. The same year the Concordat was passed, he reorganized the entire French school system, from elementary schools to universities. Napoléon's motivation for such a major overhaul of the education system was not a love of learning—he had a decidedly anti-intellectual streak—but because he believed education was a tool to mold young minds into compliant citizens. In his view, if the government could control the information taught to children, then they would grow up to be loyal and obedient citizens. This would make school the perfect training ground for future military officers, business leaders, and government functionaries. Toward that end, he centralized the educational system so that every high school (called lycée) would teach the same subjects in the same ways. Scholarships were established, but they were granted only to wealthy and middle-class students. Latin and math were the dominant subjects. Napoléon modeled the schools on the military, with students wearing uniforms and moving from one class to the next to the sound of drumbeats.

Napoléon's other dominant achievement is the Civil Code. "Better than anything else," writes French historian Roger Dufraisse, "the Civil Code symbolizes the Napoléonic stabilization of the Revolution."[11] Although the code expanded individual rights and established a much fairer judiciary, to modern eyes some of the principles of the code may seem unfair and discriminatory—such as the subjugation of wives to their husbands, the prohibition of unions and strikes, and the belief that those with more money were considered more truthful in a court of law. The effect of the Civil Code was felt far beyond France's borders. Despite its flaws, this code, still the basis for many laws throughout Europe, offered such increased personal liberties to the masses of other countries that it was as much a tool in France's conquest of other nations as was the army.

While these two policies had long-term effects on France and contributed greatly to Napoléon's historic legacy, the main concerns of the French people in 1801 were starvation and unemployment. Bread was so expensive that the poor could scarcely afford it, and the ranks of the poor were growing daily due to increasing unemployment. As a result, civil unrest threatened, and looting was widespread. Napoléon acted quickly, regulating the price of wheat and the cost of bread and increasing public-works projects that put more people to work. By the end of 1802, the crisis had passed and Napoléon's popularity was again affirmed.

FROM FIRST CONSUL FOR LIFE TO EMPEROR

While Napoléon was busy forming public policy, he did not abandon his military ambitions. Rather than remain in Paris, he personally led his troops into battle, amassing victories against and peace treaties with Austria and Russia, leaving France with no unconquered enemies left on continental Europe. The French Empire dominated Europe as no single country had since the Roman Empire. The only enemy remaining was England. Though France was still not in a position to invade England, when Napoléon gathered troops and ships on the French side of the English Channel, the English citizens panicked. Their fear probably had less to do with an invasion than with the economy since the English were suffering from unemployment and inflated prices for food, just as the French were. Napoléon's bluff worked, however, and on March 25, 1802, England and France signed the Treaty of Amiens, ending hostilities between them—though it would last only a year.

Two months later the Senate, in a public display of appreciation for the treaty, offered a ten-year renewal of Napoléon's term as first consul. Rather than being grateful for the offer, Napoléon was insulted. Once again he found the political opportunity in the situation and immediately seized it. Proclaiming that he would not accept power unless the French people conferred it on him, he called for a popular vote. But this vote was not for a mere ten-year renewal, it was to decide whether Napoléon should be named consul for life. By a vote of 3,508,895 to 8,394, Napoléon was confirmed as first consul for life.

With his power at home assured, Napoléon immediately launched his Continental System, an economic campaign meant to protect the trading of French goods through high tariffs. As part of this program, Napoléon also reinstated slavery in France's Caribbean colonies. In part, Napoléon designed his policies as economic warfare, and he hoped this program would be especially damaging to the British economy. However, the policies he implemented ended up causing more problems than they were worth: The institution of slavery caused a revolt and the loss of France's colony on Santo Domingo, Napoléon alienated European allies who were paying a heavy burden of taxes, and he goaded England into breaking the Treaty of Amiens and plunging France back into war with Great Britain, Russia, Sweden, and Austria, which were allied in what was known as the Third Coalition. England also lent its support to French royalists, who, in 1803, plotted against Napoléon. When Napoléon discovered the plot, he had the conspirators rounded up and executed.

Ironically, it was Napoléon's failure in this policy that led to his promotion. The persistence of assassination conspiracies convinced the French Senate, undoubtedly with Napoléon's help, that the only way to stop these attempted assassinations was to make the leadership of France a hereditary position. Thus, assassination would not remove the type of government, only a single person. In 1804 the Senate conferred upon

Napoléon the title of emperor, purposely avoiding the title of king, which had carried bad connotations since the French Revolution. However, this was to be a limited monarchy, with the emperor supposedly responsible to the principles of the Revolution.

Napoléon's coronation took place in 1804 in Notre Dame Cathedral in Paris and was presided over by Pope Pius VII, thus conferring the idea that Napoléon was chosen by God. Three months later the Italian Senate made Napoléon king of Italy. At the age of thirty-three, Napoléon had finally achieved his childhood ambition of becoming the modern Caesar.

RULE AS EMPEROR

Napoléon was emperor of the French Empire for ten years. These ten years were an unending parade of military battles against one international coalition after another. During this time Napoléon earned some of his greatest victories, such as the Battle of Austerlitz, and suffered some of his most severe defeats, such as those during his invasion of Russia. "Conquest has made me what I am," he said, "and conquest alone can maintain me."[12] In the end, however, the logistical problem of defending conquered territories while trying to conquer new ones proved insurmountable.

But there were also problems at home in France. Napoléon created the same kind of imperial nobility, with its accompanying favoritism, that had sparked the French Revolution. His justification was that such a traditional court helped France in its dealings with the many other monarchies throughout Europe. Nevertheless, there was grumbling from the populace.

Other moves also alienated the French people. In 1809 Napoléon sought to further legitimize his dynasty by divorcing Joséphine—whom he still loved—to marry the Austrian archduchess Marie-Louise, whom he hoped would bear him a son and heir. He also hoped that the marriage would forge an alliance with his father-in-law, the emperor Francis of Austria.

The distraction of his bustling court not only isolated Napoléon from the people, but also took its toll on his once-prodigious work schedule. As first consul, it had been common for him to work eighteen hours each day, taking only fifteen-minute breaks for meals. Sometimes he would arise in the middle of the night to work more. But this changed when he became emperor. His once skinny body grew plumper, his endurance weakened, and his interest in controlling every detail of government lessened.

NAPOLÉON'S FALL

Some of the same characteristics that brought Napoléon to power contributed to his downfall. He had always been something of a loner, contemptuous of the opinions of others. But as emperor, he became even more isolated. He replaced his more independent-minded advisers with men who only told him what he wanted to hear. Also, the ruthlessness that had served him so well in his rise through the military ranks became his main political weapon. "Abroad and at home," he admitted, "I reign only through the fear I inspire."[15] This attitude caused further alienation of the public—Napoléon's main source of political power—both in France and throughout the empire. In other countries under Napoléon's control, this dissatisfaction spawned a growing nationalism and rejection of the French way of life.

Napoléon's economic policy fared no better. The Continental System, which he had designed to reduce England's economic influence and to create more demand for French goods, was ineffective. Although there was more of a demand in France for French goods, the French were unable to meet this demand. With more demand than supply, prices rose so high that smuggling contraband became a thriving business. In the meantime, economies of countries throughout the French Empire were suffering severely. It was inevitable that, just to survive, hard-hit countries within the French Empire would have to turn against France.

In the past Napoléon had been able to recover from political setbacks by mounting successful military campaigns. However, Napoléon, once the most feared military commander in the world, began to suffer significant defeats. In 1812 he marched into Russia with nearly half a million men, only to be forced into a hasty retreat by a harsh winter and lack of supplies. Only about four thousand of his soldiers survived. The following year, with his army rebuilt, he faced a powerful Austrian army of five hundred thousand, which shredded his troops. Another defeat at the hands of the English forced him to give up Spain. Other territories were also lost, and France, with its troops exhausted and decimated, could do little to prevent it.

Seeing their enemy weakened, an alliance of Austria,

Poland, Prussia, Sweden, England, and Russia invaded France. Napoléon knew that his defeat would mean his removal from power, so he rallied the troops and prepared to march against the invaders. However, his own marshals refused to fight, giving Napoléon no choice but to abdicate. Said one marshal, "Did [Napoléon] imagine that after he had endowed us with lands, titles, and income that we would then get ourselves killed for him? It's his own fault: he made life too easy for us."[14] The betrayal of his closest marshals, the refusal of his wife to join him in Paris, and his humiliating abdication led Napoléon to attempt suicide. He swallowed poison that he had been carrying with him since the retreat from Russia, but time had diluted the poison's strength. Napoléon suffered painful convulsions but lived.

In 1814 Napoléon was stripped of his title and was exiled to the rugged island of Elba, off the coast of Italy. There he was to be the sovereign ruler, with an income of nearly $2 million, a household staff, seven hundred soldiers from his Old Guard, and a large home. Though Napoléon tried to busy himself with governing Elba, he quickly grew bored and depressed. His wife refused to bring their son and join him in exile. The British press even referred to him as a dead man. At age forty-five, Napoléon Bonaparte had conquered much of the world—only to lose it all and become nothing more than a common joke and the subject of satiric cartoons.

THE RETURN TO POWER

The next grand scheme in Napoléon's life, known as the Hundred Days, is significant more because of its romantic appeal than its political impact. Despite his exile, Napoléon kept a sharp eye on the political maneuverings in Paris as well as in the rest of Europe. The French monarchy had been restored, and he realized that Louis XVIII—the Bourbon king—was making himself very unpopular. Once again nobility was favored over merit, army officers were forced to retire at half pay, and the Catholic Church was regaining its influence. The principles of the French Revolution seemed to have been betrayed. In addition to political missteps, the French government made the mistake of alienating the former emperor by refusing to pay the pensions it owed Napoléon and his family. Napoléon's mother encouraged him to take action, telling him that it would better if he were to die on the battlefield than to live out such a paltry existence on Elba.

On March 1, 1815, Napoléon sneaked back into France and began his bloodless campaign to recapture his empire. Twenty days later, having gathered loyal troops along the way, he marched into Paris and reclaimed power—without ever having fired a shot. Louis XVIII had fled the city the night before.

This time, Napoléon's rule did not go smoothly. His efforts to reconcile the interests of the nobility and those of the common people failed to satisfy either. Royalist rebellions broke out and he was forced to send the army in to quell them. Seeing that France's enemies were poised to invade, Napoléon led his army into Belgium, where the combined forces of the English, Dutch, Belgian, German, and Prussian armies under England's duke of Wellington crushed Napoléon's troops at Waterloo. Three months after returning to France, Napoléon again abdicated. This time he was exiled to the much harsher and more remote island of St. Helena.

FINAL EXILE

He remained on St. Helena for five and a half years, living a reclusive life, dictating his memoirs, and enduring his declining health. Then, on May 5, 1821, at the age of fifty-one, Napoléon died. Controversy over the cause of death remains, though analysis of his hair follicles in 1995 by various investigators, including forensic scientists from the Federal Bureau of Investigation, strongly suggests that he was poisoned with arsenic. After surviving all of the assassination attempts and all of the bloody battles, Napoléon was most likely killed by a close companion, Charles Tristan de Montholon. The motive was money. Napoléon had bequeathed a sizable amount of money to de Montholon, who was deeply in debt. By killing Napoléon, he could be free of debt and free to leave St. Helena.

Napoléon was buried on St. Helena with much ceremony. In 1840, almost twenty years after his death, his remains were returned to Paris.

NAPOLÉON'S "RIGHTFUL DUE"

The story of Napoléon Bonaparte—a skinny Corsican boy who became the most powerful man in the world—has the same legendary appeal as the tale of King Arthur or the biblical story of Moses. Napoléon himself was aware of the power of legend and did his best throughout his life to perpetuate his own mythology. Stories were publicly circulated about how hard he worked, his simple manner of dress, his Spartan tastes—all designed to create the image of a leader whom people would wish to follow. Even his memoirs, written while he was in exile on St. Helena, seemed designed more to perpetuate his legend than to shed light on a complex man in complex times.

This volume of Greenhaven's People Who Made History allows the reader to see the real man behind the carefully constructed image. It explores the family influences on the young Napoléon, who was born into a culture dedicated to using violence to solve conflicts. It reveals the significance of the French Revolution in creating a political climate desperate for a strong and ruthless leader. Historians analyze Napoléon's domestic and foreign policies and the enormous impact they had on the rest of the world, including the expansion of the United States.

Napoléon held power for nearly fifteen years; during that time he was at war for all but fourteen months. This anthology also explores Napoléon as military strategist and innovator, examining individual battles to see why he became the most-studied general in history. Finally, the book examines the impact of Napoléon, separating legend from legacy. Reflecting on his life, Napoléon once said, "For all the attempts to restrict, suppress and muffle me, it will be difficult to make me disappear completely. French historians will have to deal with the Empire . . . and will have to give me my rightful due."[15]

NOTES

1. Robert B. Holtman, *The Napoléonic Revolution.* Baton Rouge: Louisiana State University Press, 1967, p. 7.

2. J. Christopher Herold, ed., *The Age of Napoléon.* New York: American Heritage, 1963, p. 412.

3. Quoted in F.M.H. Markham, *Napoléon and the Awakening of Europe.* London: English Universities Press, 1961, p. 9.

4. Quoted in Markham, *Napoléon and the Awakening of Europe,* p. 10.

5. Quoted in J. Christopher Herold, ed. and trans., *The Mind of Napoléon: A Selection from His Written and Spoken Words.* New York: Columbia University Press, 1955, p. 43.

6. Quoted in Markham, *Napoléon and the Awakening of Europe,* p. 14.

7. Quoted in Roger Dufraisse, *Napoléon*, trans. Steven Englund. New York: McGraw-Hill, 1992, p. 18.

8. Quoted in Dufraisse, *Napoléon*, p. 25.

9. Quoted in Markham, *Napoléon and the Awakening of Europe*, p. 35.

10. Quoted in Markham, *Napoléon and the Awakening of Europe*, p. 60.

11. Dufraisse, *Napoléon*, p. 73.

12. Quoted in Markham, *Napoléon and the Awakening of Europe*, p. 92.

13. Quoted in Markham, *Napoléon and the Awakening of Europe*, p. 92.

14. Quoted in Dufraisse, *Napoléon*, p. 145.

15. Quoted in Alan Schom, *Napoléon Bonaparte*. New York: Harper-Collins, 1997, p. 789.

CHAPTER 1

THE MAJOR INFLUENCES ON NAPOLÉON'S CHARACTER AND CAREER

The Bonaparte Family Influence

Frank McLynn

Frank McLynn is an award-winning historian and
visiting professor in the Department of Literature at
Strathclyde University, England. In the following selection taken from his book, *Napoléon: A Biography*,
McLynn suggests that the marriage of Napoléon's
parents was more like a corporate merger than a romantic liaison. Each came from a respected family
of the Corsican nobility, with both of their families
seeking an alliance through marriage that would
strengthen their social and financial positions on
Corsica. McLynn attributes Napoléon's self-discipline
and lust for power to the influence of his mother,
Letizia, who punished and ruled her children like a
dictator. In addition, the author notes, the constant
revolutionary atmosphere of Corsica instilled in
Napoléon a ruthless pragmatism that later allowed
him to achieve his grand goals of conquest, regardless of the means.

On 2 June 1764 Carlo Buonaparte of Ajaccio, an eighteen-
year-old law student, married the fourteen-year-old Marie-
Letizia Ramolino, also of Ajaccio. Both families were descended from Italian mercenaries in Genoese pay who settled
in Corsica at the beginning of the sixteenth century. . . .

A MARRIAGE OF CONVENIENCE

The marriage of Carlo and Letizia was a solid, down-to-
earth marriage of convenience. There is even reason to believe that Carlo hedged his bets by not marrying in the
Church in 1764, or ever. It was well known that Corsicans
took an idiosyncratic, eclectic attitude to the Catholic
Church, which was why legal marriage on the island con-

sisted in the agreement of the two male heads of families, the signature of a dotal contract, and the act of consummation. The likelihood is that Carlo simply refused to go through with a religious ceremony, and for reasons of pride and saving face the two clans kept quiet about it.

Again, contrary to the mythmaking, it is untrue that some of the Ramolinos opposed the match for political reasons, allegedly on the grounds that they supported the Genoese masters of the island while the Buonapartes backed the independence movement under Pasquale Paoli. Almost certainly, they simply had doubts that this was the very best dynastic bargain they could strike while, as for political ideology, both the Buonapartes and Ramolinos were notorious trimmers who made obeisance to whichever party in Corsica had the most power.

Carlo, a tall young man with a prominent nose, sensual lips and almond-shaped eyes, was a hedonist and sensualist. Cunning, self-regarding, unrefined, unscrupulous, he made it clear that his marriage was no love match by declaring a preference for a girl of the Forcioli family. The romancers claim that he was bowled over by Letizia's beauty, but portraits reveal a woman whose mouth was too small, whose nose was too long and whose face was too austere for a claim to real beauty to be advanced. It was true that she was petite (5'1"), with rich dark-brown hair and slender white hands; and what she had, incontestably and by common consent, were large, lustrous, deep-set eyes. As was normal at the time, Letizia was wholly uneducated and trained in nothing but domestic skills.

Letizia fulfilled the essential requirement of women of the time, which was to be an efficient childbearer. She gave birth to thirteen children in all, of whom eight survived. A son, named Napoléon, was born and died in 1765. Pregnant again almost immediately, Letizia next brought forth a girl who also died. Then came a mysterious interlude of about two years. Allegedly Paoli sent the twenty-year-old Carlo as his envoy to Rome, to appease the Pope when he launched his planned attack on the Genoese island of Capraia (Capraia and Genoa had originally been deeded to Genoa by papal gift), but the best evidence shows Carlo becoming a Paolista while he was in Italy. Carlo's time in Rome seems to have been spent in cohabitation with a married woman. His own story was that he returned from Rome after running out of funds, but a stronger tradition has it that he seduced a virgin and was run out of town. On his return to Corsica he again impregnated Letizia, who this time bore him a lusty son in the shape of Joseph (originally named Giuseppe), who was born on 7 July 1768.

THE FAMILY FINANCES

Another prevalent myth about Napoléon's background was that he was born into indigence. The property brought into the marriage by Carlo and Letizia seems to have been nicely calculated, since Letizia's dowry was valued at 6,750 livres and Carlo's assets at about 7,000 livres. The joint capital generated an annual income of about 670 livres or about £9,000 [$14,600] a year in today's [1997] money. In addition, there was the money earned by Carlo. Pasquale Paoli employed the young man as his secretary on account of his unusually neat and clear handwriting. Carlo also worked as a *procureur*—approximately equivalent to a British solicitor. Letizia employed two servants and a wet-nurse—hardly badges of poverty.

What Carlo and Letizia suffered from was not poverty but relative deprivation. The Buonapartes and their great rivals, the Pozzo di Borgos, were among the richest families in Ajaccio, but they were aware that they were big fish in a very small pond. Across the water, in mainland France, their wealth would have counted for nothing and their pretensions to nobility would have been laughed at. The Buonapartes wanted to be as rich as the richest nobles in France and, since they could not be, they created a compensatory myth of dire poverty. Economic conditions in Corsica and their own pretensions worked against them. A sharecropping economy based on vineyards and a primitive barter system meant there were few opportunities for generating a surplus, hence no possibility for profits and making money. Even if there had been, Carlo Buonaparte's aspirations to noble status stood in the way, for to a noble the Church, the Law and the Army were the only acceptable professions, and even the lower reaches of the Law, such as Carlo's position as *procureur*, were essentially beyond the aristocratic pale.

Napoléon was often, to his fury, called 'the Corsican'. He always denied that his birthplace had any significance, but no human being can slough off early environmental and geographical influences just by say-so. The restlessness in

Napoléon's later character must owe something to the confused and chaotic politics of the island, which he imbibed with his mother's milk, or rather that of his wet-nurse. As Dorothy Carrington has written: 'defeat, resistance, betrayal, heroism, torture, execution and conspiracy were the topics of the first conversations he overheard. Conversations that left a permanent imprint on his mind.' . . .

NAPOLÉON'S VOLATILE CHILDHOOD

There is little hard evidence for the events of Napoléon's early boyhood. There is a strong tradition that he was sent in 1773 to a school for girls run by nuns and that he was the terror of the playground. . . .

It is certain that at about the age of seven he was sent to a Jesuit school, where he learned to read and write, to do sums and take in the rudiments of Latin and ancient history. But stories of tantrums and of a systematically destructive boy who pulled the stuffing out of chairs, wrecked plants and deliberately cut grooves in tables were later accretions bruited about by his enemies and are fairly obvious attempts to read back into his childhood authenticated adult traits.

Three items of anecdotal evidence relating to these early years seem to be genuinely grounded in fact, not least because Letizia and Joseph vouched for them in old age. Letizia recalled that when she gave her children paints to use on the wall of their playroom, all the other children painted puppets but Napoléon alone painted soldiers. Joseph recalled that at school, when they played Romans and Carthaginians, Napoléon was chosen by the teacher to be a Carthaginian while Joseph was a Roman. Wanting to be on the winning side, Napoléon nagged and wheedled at the teacher until the roles were reversed and he could play the Roman. This would square with the tradition, which seems solidly grounded, that Napoléon picked on Joseph, fought with him at every opportunity and generally tried to browbeat and bully him. Joseph was quiet and mild, but Napoléon was rumbustious and belligerent.

Finally, there is Letizia's testimony that she was a stickler for the truth while Napoléon showed early signs of being a pathological liar. This was part of a general clash of wills between mother and son which saw Letizia frequently having recourse to the whip. Carlo spoiled his children, but Letizia was a fearsome martinet with a rather masculine nature and a natural love of power. A stern taskmistress who always punished for the slightest fault, Letizia laid about her with gusto when her second son misbehaved. She drove him to Mass with slaps and blows, whipped him when he stole fruit, misbehaved in church or—on one notorious occasion— laughed at a crippled grandmother. Letizia was also cunning and devious. When her son was eight and an altar boy, she vowed to mete out punishment for his less than reverent behaviour on the altar, but faced the problem that she would find it hard to lay hands on the agile and fully-clothed Napoléon. To lull his suspicions, she told him she would not beat him for his offence. But when he took his clothes off she pounced on him with the whip.

NAPOLÉON AS PSYCHOPATH

In this excerpt from Alan Schom's Napoléon Bonaparte, *the author asserts that Napoléon's behavior falls within the technical definition of a psychopath. He lists the characteristics of psychopathic behavior, and gives an example of his sometimes extreme and erratic behavior.*

From a psychiatric viewpoint, all my medical friends confirm that Bonaparte—like so many dictatorial rulers—would, according to the U.K. Mental Health Act of 1983, be described as a psychopath, a term that includes in its definition:

a. Failure to make loving relationships

b. A propensity toward highly impulsive, irrational actions

c. Lack of sense of guilt or sensitivity for own actions

d. Failure to learn from adverse experiences

The combination of all four traits is reflected by the various kidnappings, murders, lies, and wars he perpetrated to the very end.

Napoléon was also very paranoid long before coming to power, even as a child. Indeed, in addition to having servants first taste all food and drink presented, when General [Paul-Charles] Thiébault, his loyal new military governor of a recently confiscated Rhineland state, sent him several thousand bottles of choice wines he had just seized, Napoléon wrote back angrily adominishing him for wanting to poison him and ordered every bottle broken.

Alan Schom, *Napoléon Bonaparte*, 1997.

Napoléon never cried out under the lash, but fear and respect for his mother replaced genuine love. Napoléon resented her doctrinaire principles and her sacrifice of reality for appearances. A true Latin, Letizia believed that outward show was the most important thing and that it was better to go without food so as to be able to wear a smart suit. Naturally austere and penny-pinching, she had no qualms about sending her children to bed hungry, both because she thought such hardship was good for them and because she genuinely preferred to spend the money on furnishing the house and keeping up appearances. Superficially, at least, the challenge and response between mother and son worked out well, since Napoléon did learn the value of discipline; his siblings, by contrast, were notorious for the lack of it. Napoléon's testimony to his mother on St Helena is the truth, but it is not the whole truth: 'I owe her a great deal. She instilled into me pride and taught me good sense.' . . .

THE CORSICAN LEGACY

The Corsican legacy may partly account for the ruthless pragmatism in Napoléon's personality, the impatience with abstract theory and the conviction that, ultimately, human problems are solved by main force. There is also the 'primitive' aspect of the adult Napoléon, frequently noticed by memorialists and biographers. The psychoanalyst A.A. Brill wrote: 'There is no doubt that Napoléon represents the very acme of primitivity,' and went on to argue that his universal fascination lies in his embodiment of those primitive qualities we can scarcely acknowledge consciously in 'civilized' society. This is not so very strange when we consider the backward and primitive nature of eighteenth-century Corsican life, where even the everyday sights, smells and sounds were primordial. Contemporary accounts speak of the streets of Ajaccio as suffused with the stench of animals slaughtered outside butchers' shops and the animal hides stretched out to tan in the sun. The noisome foetor in the streets was exacerbated by the clouds of flies, the stifling summer climate, and the acute shortage of water. There are grounds for believing that Napoléon's later addiction to lying in hot baths was compensation for a childhood marked by water shortage.

The other quintessentially primitive aspect of Corsica, noted by all travellers and visitors to the island, was the

As lieutenant-colonel of the first battalion of Corsica, Napoléon was exposed to the Corsican legacy of ruthless pragmatism and the use of force to solve human problems.

vendetta. The tradition of blood vengeance was handed down to the seventh generation, and a girl had the number of her cousins reckoned as part of her dowry so that wrongs done to the clan would never be forgotten; the males in the clan refused to shave and went about bearded until the affront to the family honour was avenged. It was this aspect of the Corsicans that *ancien régime* statesmen like the duc de Choiseul particularly hated. Rousseau, Boswell and other admirers might praise the Corsicans as shrewd, verbose, voluble, highly intelligent and as interested in politics as the inhabitants of an ancient Greek city-state. But against this, said the critics, was the fact that the Corsicans were also proud, prickly, arrogant, vindictive, unforgiving, implacable, vengeful and alarmingly quick to take offence or construe words and actions as insults.

The institution of vendetta knew no boundaries of class or status, only of family and clan. Napoléon himself clearly surmounted the tradition of vendetta, as he always killed his enemies for reasons of state not out of personal grievance; indeed he can be faulted for being absurdly tolerant of inveterate personal enemies. His enemies in Corsica, however, did not have his forbearance: the rival family of Pozzo di Borgo pursued the Buonapartes with vendetta to Napoléon's grave and beyond. They intrigued with his enemies, manipulated Czar Alexander and were among the first to suggest St Helena as a place of exile. Only after the fall of Louis-Napoléon in 1870 and the death of the Prince Imperial in the Zulu War of 1879 did the Pozzo di Borgos relax and build the castle of LaPunta as a monument to their final victory.

FAMILY INFLUENCE

Far more important than the influence of Corsica on Napoléon was the impact of his family. It is quite clear from his later career, as indeed from the tenuous record of his first nine years, that Napoléon was obsessed by rivalry with Joseph and yearned to supplant him. The later political history of Napoléon the emperor is sometimes inexplicable without taking into account his 'Joseph complex'. In later years Napoléon indulged his elder brother shamelessly, leading one to conclude that the childhood hatred must have been compensated and the original aggression visited on others. It was this consideration that led Freud to write: 'To push Joseph aside, to take his place, to become Joseph himself, must have been the little Napoléon's strongest emotion. . . . Hundreds of thousands of strangers had to pay the penalty of this little fiend's having spared his first enemy.' The early feelings of hostility towards his brother may well have been compounded, in Napoléon's unconscious, by the idea that he was a 'replacement child' for the first Napoléon, who died in 1765; Joseph, therefore, had a clear identity and a clear focus in his parents' affections which he, as a 'substitute', did not have.

Towards his father Napoléon always evinced an ambivalence characterized by contempt for the real man coupled with idolization of Carlo or a Platonic form of Carlo; this maybe found expression ultimately in Napoléon's desire to be a second great French Emperor, the first being Charlemagne who, bearing the same Christian name as his father, was the ideal-type. Consciously, Napoléon disliked his father's extravagance and addiction to pleasure, but was proud of him as a patriot and Paolista. Yet it is universally conceded that during Napoléon's early life Carlo was a shadowy figure. The really important early parental influence came from his mother.

Some of the mistakes attributed to Letizia probably did not have the consequences ascribed to them. Wilhelm Reich speculated, from the mixture of great energy and passive tendencies, that Napoléon might have been a 'phallic-narcissistic' character, as a result of an 'overfeminized' early socialization, with the nuns at school and the overbearing Letizia at home. It is, however, unlikely that his brief attendance at the nuns' school had any significant role in his formation, and it is surely farfetched to imagine Letizia's beatings as the genesis of sado-masochistic tendencies. However, the general thesis of an unconscious desire for revenge against the opposite sex seems well grounded in the evidence of his later life. In particular, he always thought of women as being totally without honour, duplicitous, deceivers, liars.

In later life Napoléon always showered lavish praise on his mother in public or when talking to inferiors. To intimates and confidantes it was a different story, for then he allowed himself to express his darker feelings about Letizia. In theory her meanness with money should have balanced Carlo's extravagance but the adult Napoléon felt, though he would obviously not have used the term, that both his parents were neurotic in countervailing and fissiparous ways. He hated the way his mother got him to spy on Carlo when he was drinking and gambling in the Ajaccio saloons. There were also more sinister suspicions about Letizia and [the governor of Corsica, the Comte de] Marbeuf [that they were having an affair] that he dared not express consciously. But it is important to be clear that Napoléon's ambivalence about his mother was part of a general obsession with Letizia, and we would therefore be justified in adding 'mother fixation' to the other 'complexes' already noted.

All human beings struggle in vain against the determinism of the parental legacy, both biological and psychological. The curious paradox of being a charismatic workaholic, which was the character of the adult Napoléon, surely results from the very different and centrifugal qualities of his two ill-matched parents. From Carlo he would appear to have derived the histrionic and magnetic qualities, the self-dramatization and the ability to win men; from Letizia came the self-discipline and the fanatical devotion to work. It was the Letizia-derived qualities that would be most valuable to him during his virtual orphancy at Brienne.

The French Revolution

George Gordon Andrews

One of the most vigorously debated issues regarding Napoléon is whether he was the savior or the executioner of the ideals of the French Revolution. George Gordon Andrews, in the following passage from his book, *Napoléon in Review*, discusses the effect of the Revolution on Napoléon's rise and rule. Napoléon's phenomenal rise from his modest beginnings would have been impossible, contends Andrews, if not for the French Revolution's legacy of "advancement by merit" rather than by importance of family connections. But even more important, he notes, was the French Revolution's influence on the many social and military innovations that are considered to be Napoléon's greatest achievements, including his foreign policy, educational reforms, civil code, and religious policies. Andrews was a history professor at the University of Iowa.

[German writer Johann Wolfgang von] Goethe once remarked: "To make an epoch in the world two conditions are notoriously essential—a good head and a great inheritance. Napoléon inherited the French Revolution." The greatest bequest of the Revolution to Napoléon, at least from a personal point of view, was one laid at the door of every Frenchman—the opportunity to reach the highest position to which his talents and energy entitled him. Napoléon was not the originator of "the career open to talent"; he was only developing a program which the Revolution had made possible and to which he himself was in large part indebted for his rise to power.

In the old regime the door of opportunity was closed to the commoner and to the impoverished noble. The best positions in the government and the army were open only to the privileged few. There might be an occasional exception, but it merely proved the rule. Entrance into the ranks of the nobility of the robe could be secured by purchase, it is true; but that required wealth. "Of the thirty-six persons who held portfolios between 1774 and 1789, there was only one [Necker, and he was wealthy] who was not noble. . . . Contrary to what is often alleged, even the intendants, who were responsible for the administration of the provinces, were no longer chosen among men of low birth. All those who held office under Louis XVI belonged to noble or recently ennobled families, sometimes of some generations' standing." In the Church the situation was the same. There was nothing in theory against a humble priest becoming an abbot or bishop, or even ascending the chair of St. Peter. But the theory was about all that remained of this democratic tendency. "In 1789 there was not one of the 143 bishops who was not a nobleman." What hope was there for the nonprivileged classes of France under such conditions? The Revolution shattered the citadel of privilege and opened the doors of opportunity. But for the Revolution, it is not unreasonable to believe that Napoléon might have remained a minor artillery officer lost in the obscurity of some provincial post.

The watchwords of the Revolution were *liberty, equality,* and *fraternity.* If the first of these was most often in the mouths of the politicians, the second was more deeply implanted in the hearts of the people. The desire for civil and social equality was widespread and urgent among the French, and Napoléon was quick to realize its significance. He told Madame de Rémusat that equality was the only serious demand of the people. "The secret of all your vanities is that anyone may rise where all are equal. It is therefore essential that everyone be given the hope of advancing himself. . . . Vanity has both made and ended the Revolution. Liberty is a pretext. Equality is all the rage with you and that is why the people are content with a king taken from the ranks of the soldiers." Napoléon knew the tremendous appeal which equality made to the masses; but, better still, he had put the principle to the test in his own experience and found it good. Equality of opportunity or the career open to talent was appropriated and made a permanent part of his system.

THE REVOLUTION TRANSFORMS THE MILITARY

The Revolution had likewise wrought a radical transformation in military operations. Frederick the Great [of Prussia] was the ideal of the militarists of the old school, but even here the spirit of the man had been lost and only the empty shell of his formal tactics remained. The movements were slow, methodical, and cumbersome. Great stress was placed upon precision and rigid formations. Much time was spent in manœuvring for position. Every effort was made to preserve the army and reduce losses to a minimum. But perhaps most important of all, the soldiers themselves were without spirit or zeal, largely owing to an iron discipline maintained by corporal punishment. The Revolution changed all this. First of all it provided an army fired with aggressive patriotism and contagious enthusiasm. Flogging was abolished. As a consequence discipline was at first relaxed, but out of it grew an individual initiative that made the revolutionary soldier far superior to the old type. In larger operations the gaining of an objective became all important. If there were more effective means than the old orthodox methods and formations, use them. The rigid massed formations were abandoned as a result and lines of skirmishers were thrown out which were followed by the attacking columns. Artillery and cavalry were made more effective, especially the latter, in the overthrow and pursuit of a weakened enemy. Rapid marches and surprise attacks supplanted the old slow movements. And in a country so well supplied with zealous soldiers it was not necessary to be so saving of men. Victory was the essential and losses were not an unreasonable price to pay for it.

These changes had been brought about gradually and in a somewhat fumbling manner, but they had already produced remarkable results before Napoléon was given command of the army of Italy. . . . This new and efficient military system with its enticing promise was ready for use when Napoléon came upon the scene, and from the very first he handled it with the assurance and finesse of a master. He won the battle of Ulm, virtually without fighting, by skilfully executed forced marches which cut General [Charles] Mack off from retreat and forced him to surrender without striking a blow. These brilliant tactics inspired the epigram: "Our Emperor makes war not with our arms but with our legs." Along with the military machine came also the military tradition—dependence upon the army, confidence in its ability and right in the last resort to settle both the internal and the external affairs of the State.

NAPOLÉON INHERITS A FOREIGN POLICY OF CONQUEST

Closely associated with his military inheritance and to a great degree dependent upon it for realization was the ambitious program of the Revolution itself. Napoléon has been condemned most often perhaps for his ambition. That he was ambitious no one would deny and he himself admitted it on occasion. But that his ambition was entirely personal, that he alone was responsible for it, and that the struggle of France for universal dominion was due solely to his insatiable greed for power is a serious misstatement of the case. The National Assembly had indeed put itself on record as opposed to aggression. In the session of May 22, 1790 it had decreed "that the French nation renounces the undertaking of any war with the object of making conquests, and that it will never employ its forces against the liberty of any people." But the revolutionary program was a missionary one. It declared and urged the rights of man and the sovereignty of the people. . . . The supporters of the Revolution hoped and expected to make conquests in this cause. The conquering agency at this time, however, was intended to be ideas and not armies. Armies, notwithstanding, have been enlisted not infrequently in the support of ideas, and the transition from this policy of nonintervention to conquest is one of the most significant developments of the Revolution.

The steps in this transition are more or less logically implied in the basic program. To point them out with typical examples of their operation in practice will make the development clearer. When a neighbouring people was converted to revolutionary principles, it was only natural that they should seek to secure the advantages of such principles by overthrowing their old oppressive government and institutions. This was done by the people in the Papal territory of Avignon and by the inhabitants of Savoy. The French found it both logical and advantageous to encourage and approve of these changes. There could be only commendation for following the French example in asserting the inalienable right to freedom from oppression. But having gained their freedom, these peoples feared that they might lose it again, and they requested annexation to France. Here again there was no violation of the principle of the sovereignty of the people, but there were some serious, if not dangerous, possibilities involved. The former ruler might attempt to reconquer his people. Was France ready to go to war to protect them from their oppressor? This might be no difficult task in the case of a weak power, but what if the request should come from a people ruled by one of the great powers of Europe? And, since France approved of freedom, how far should she go in helping an oppressed people shake off their fetters? Should she give military assistance?

Her enthusiasm for the cause soon led her into a veritable propaganda crusade with its attendant responsibilities. As [French historian Albert] Mathiez puts it: "By calling upon the peoples to revolt, republican France had entered into moral obligations towards them which she could not evade. Her propaganda logically involved the protection of those who had revolted; and was not annexation the best protection she could afford them?" Furthermore, if governments continued to fall as a result of the influence of French principles, would not the old monarchies combine against France in a struggle for existence? That this possibility was recognized is clear from the words of Danton: "While it is our duty to give liberty to neighbouring peoples, I declare that we have the right to say to them: 'You shall have no more kings, for, so long as you are surrounded by tyrants, a coalition of them may imperil our own liberty.'"

A DELICATE PROBLEM

But there was yet another aspect to the problem. Some people would always remain loyal to their old governments. When France took the field in the cause of freedom, what if the majority of the people were so blind to their own interests as to support their rulers or refuse the blessings of liberty? This was the situation that developed in the Austrian Netherlands. Whatever love the Belgians may have had for French principles at first was turned into hatred by the heavy war requisitions levied upon the country. They were glad to see the Austrians go, but they wanted neither annexation to France nor French institutions.

Even before this the National Convention had issued a declaration of "fraternity and assistance to all peoples who shall wish to recover their liberty, and charges the executive power to give to the generals the necessary orders to furnish assistance to these peoples and to defend the citizens who may have been or who may be harassed for the cause of liberty." Conditions in the Netherlands, however, called for something more explicit and it came in the famous decree of December

15, 1792. "In the countries which are or shall be occupied by the armies of the Republic, the generals shall proclaim immediately, in the name of the French nation, the sovereignty of the people, the suppression of all the established authorities and [privileged institutions]. . . . They shall announce to the people . . . that they will convoke them directly in primary or communal assemblies in order to create and organize an administration. . . . There shall be made a list of the expenses which the French Republic shall have incurred for the common defence and of the sums which it may have received, and the French nation shall make arrangements with the government which shall have been established for that which may be due. . . . The French nation declares that it will treat as enemies the people who, refusing liberty and equality, or renouncing them, may wish to preserve, recall, or treat with the prince and the privileged castes."

The distinction between the incorporation of peoples liberated against their wishes and conquest was indeed a delicate one. The governments of Europe were no doubt justified in refusing to recognize it. The Directory followed the same policy by continuing the war and setting up the so-called "encircling republics." Napoléon was initiated into the mysteries of high diplomacy in these enterprises. The Revolution had become definitely committed to a policy of expansion and conquest. This policy was inherited by Napoléon. He neither originated it nor did he personally influence it in its formative stages. That he found it congenial to his spirit, exploited it to his personal advantage, and developed it to an extent only possible to a master of war, there can be no doubt. But he retained to the last the revolutionary obsession that in extending the rule of France and establishing enlightened institutions among conquered peoples, he was conferring upon them an incomparable benefit.

THE FOUNDATIONS FOR EDUCATION REFORM

Napoléon is often given great credit for establishing a national system of education in France, but here again he built upon foundations laid by the Revolution. According to the *cahiers* [a report prepared by the French State-General], criticism of the existing educational system was general before 1789. The lack of schools was deplored. In such schools as there were, the teachers were declared to be incompetent and the studies of little or no value. The demand for reform came from all classes. The nobility of Saint–Mihiel [a small town in northeastern France] even went so far as to say that "national education is perhaps the most important problem which the Estates General shall have to consider." That the Constituent Assembly accomplished so little in this line was no doubt due to the pressure of other duties and the widely divergent opinions as to what should be done. . . .

Napoléon built upon the foundations laid by the National Convention, but the structure he raised took the form which he considered most necessary for the welfare and preservation of the State.

THE FOUNDATIONS FOR RELIGIOUS REFORM

His solution of the religious problem is equally significant in this connexion. A great deal has been written about the religious aspect of the Revolution and the attitude and aims of the revolutionary leaders regarding it. There were, no doubt, many factors involved in this intricate problem. One of the most important was certainly the financial. The property of the Church, the tithe, and other dues came up for discussion and criticism early in the movement and remained an essential consideration to the end. On the more religious side, the revolutionary attitude is most clearly revealed in the Civil Constitution of the Clergy decreed on July 12, 1790. The fact that the word "civil" was used in qualifying the title indicates the outward intention at least not to interfere with the "religious" activities of the clergy. In the very nature of the case, however, the dividing line between the civil and religious affairs of the clergy was a hazy one, and it is not surprising that in certain instances it was overstepped. Opinions differed and perhaps the outcome was inevitable. In general the framers of the Civil Constitution appear to have had in mind two fundamental purposes. The first was to reduce the independent influence of the Church and transform it into a powerful bulwark of the State. If it was not an attempt to make a religion of patriotism, it was at least an attempt to make religion patriotic and national. The second, in part growing out of the first, was an effort to destroy the effective jurisdiction of the Pope. Both of these objectives hark back to the old royal Gallicanism [devotion to French culture and tradition] enunciated in the famous Declaration of 1682. . . .

The fundamental objection to religion was not that it was Christian but that it was antinational. When, therefore, national interests were no longer in danger, the oppression of the Church gradually relaxed and education took the place of force. Liberty of worship was decreed; State support of religion was discontinued; the churches were restored to the faithful; and a general policy of secularization was inaugurated.

NAPOLÉON'S SOLUTION

Such was the condition of affairs when Napoléon came upon the scene. What was his solution of the problem? Undoubtedly he was convinced that even if the rural masses had been somewhat indifferent to the attack on Christianity, they would be at least equally indifferent to the restoration of the old faith, if they did not actually welcome it. It would win the clergy completely, especially if a reconciliation with the Pope could be effected, and their influence was important. Moreover, the old faith, if it could be kept in hand, was much more in harmony with the system which he sought to establish. He was quite aware that its restoration would be opposed by the secular, philosophic, and free-thinking class. These considerations were no doubt in his mind when he negotiated the famous Concordat of 1801 with the Pope.

It is often asserted that Napoléon overthrew the religious work of the Revolution and restored Roman Catholicism, but this is a superficial view of the settlement. Catholicism was recognized not as "the religion of the State" but as "the religion of the great majority of French citizens." The Pope relinquished all rights to the alienated ecclesiastical estates. Bishops were to be appointed by the First Consul [Napoléon], although instituted by the Pope. Curés were to be appointed by the bishops. The sword of Damocles was suspended over the Church by the provision that "its worship shall be public, and *in conformity with the police regulations which the government shall deem necessary* for the public tranquillity" (italics mine). . . .

Thus, in the Concordat, Napoléon remained true to one of the first principles of the Revolution—that is, to reduce the independent influence of the Church and develop it into a powerful support of the government and nation. It was a great nationalistic principle to which he could and did subscribe. His attitude toward the Pope reveals a further adherence to this same principle. As the Church in France was to devote itself to the service of the State, so there must be no foreign meddling in the affairs of that Church which might work to the disadvantage of the nation, not even by the head of the universal Church. In view of the powerful position which Napoléon held in Italy at this time, he doubtless also considered the possibility of dominating the policy of the Pope and using him in the furtherance of his own influence in Europe.

CODES OF NAPOLÉON

Perhaps none of the achievements of Napoléon proved more permanent and more far-reaching in its influence than his famous Codes. Of these the best and most important was the Civil Code. The idea of a unified system of laws for France was, of course, not original with Napoléon. It far antedated even the Revolution. But the Revolution revived and stimulated the movement and provided the most favourable opportunity for its realization. The old French law reached back for its beginnings chiefly to German and Roman sources. From these had come many modifications and amalgamations due to local conditions and temporary vicissitudes until the differing codes in the country before the Revolution were numbered in the hundreds. What was legal in one place might be illegal across a local boundary a few leagues away. To add to the confusion between the legal and illegal was the generally recognized principle that the king was the source of all law. The law, then, was at the mercy of the arbitrary will of the sovereign. This principle had been aptly phrased in the old maxim: "As wills the king, so wills the law." The Revolution was in part a protest against this conflict of laws and arbitrary government. The revolutionary attitude on the latter point was well put by the journalist Le Hodey when he declared that the time had come at last to reverse the old maxim and to say: "As wills the law, so wills the king."

The demand for a reign of law, therefore, was general in the early Revolution. But it was for a uniform system, applicable to the whole of France, which would be in harmony with the enlightenment of the century and not subject to the whim of any potentate. . . .

THE SPIRIT OF THE FRENCH REVOLUTION

The unifying and nationalizing of France was a great ideal which was given a mighty impulse, if it was not actually created, by the Revolution. Napoléon accepted it with all his heart. By a policy of reconciliation with a State-subordinated

Church, by a uniform code of laws, and by a State-controlled system of education he sought to make it a reality. Not that he was actuated alone by a deep and abiding love for France. The national ideal was not to be an end in itself. As the enlightenment and progress of the Revolution was to expand over ever widening circles of humanity, so France, with its Revolution purified and organized by his surpassing intelligence, was to be the agent in the accomplishment of this supreme purpose. He sought to build up the French nation in order that he might use it along with all other effective means in extending the beneficent influence of the Revolution under his own power.

Not only in the cases cited did Napoléon build upon revolutionary foundations, but in many of his other projects he attempted what had been considered previously by the National Convention and the Directory. According to Fournier,

> During the summer of 1795 France was not only intending to land an army in the British Isles but also to destroy England by closing all European ports against her commerce. Here, therefore, was Napoléon's continental blockade already shadowed forth. Even in his Oriental plans the authorities at Paris had preceded him. At the time the landing in England was being planned, and long before Napoléon had dreamt of outrivalling Alexander [the Great, Fourth century B.C. Greek ruler and renowned military strategist], the Directory had Britain's sources of wealth in India under consideration. . . . In like manner during the last ten years of the century we find the policy to be pursued towards Germany mapped out point by point, exactly as it was afterwards accomplished by Napoléon. The idea of the secularization of the German ecclesiastical principalities had already been mooted under the Convention in 1795. . . . In the diplomatic records of the Committee of Public Safety and the Directory, the idea is suggested of a Confederation of the Princes of the Rhine under French protection which became fact in 1806, and likewise the design of forcing Prussia and Austria as far east as possible, so as to bring the mouths of the Weser and Elbe under France's control and thus withdraw them from that of England.

These enterprises were indeed shaped and developed by the hand of Napoléon and shot through with his genius, but they were none the less of revolutionary origin. The Revolution was for him a rich inheritance which he successfully exploited to his own advantage and to the building up of the great system which he sought to establish.

CHAPTER 2

NAPOLÉON'S DOMESTIC POLICIES

The Civil Code

Martyn Lyons

Martyn Lyons, a history professor at the University of New South Wales in Australia, has written extensively on the French Revolution and nineteenth century cultural history. He is the author of *Napoléon Bonaparte and the Legacy of the French Revolution*, from which the following is excerpted. Despite his many victories on the battlefield, Napoléon considered the formation of France's Civil Code as his greatest accomplishment. The Code abolished the regional laws which varied drastically from one section of France to the other and provided a unified legal system that treated all citizens equally. Lyons outlines the Code's major changes in property and family law, which included making divorce more difficult to obtain, marriage more secular rather than sacramental, and restricting women's rights substantially. He also describes the impact these innovations had, not just on France, but on all of Europe.

The codification of the law, and the construction of a new educational system were the most permanent achievements of the Napoléonic period. The French Revolution had shattered ancient assumptions about education, property rights, family law and individual freedoms: to Bonaparte fell the task of making a final pronouncement. His Civil Code provided a clear statement of the citizen's rights and duties, in marriage and divorce, dowries, adoption and illegitimacy, wills and inheritances.

Napoléon, looking back from exile and defeat, claimed the Civil Code as a greater victory than any he had won on the battlefield. It may seem strange that a man so devoted to speedy action and incisive conquest should be closely associated with the work of dry and meticulous legists. The Civil Code, however, known after 1807 as the Code Napoléon, bears the stamp of Bonaparte. [Leading French novelist] Stendhal was to claim he read it and reread it as a model of prose clarity. Its provisions on property, family and inheritance law consolidated the Revolution, and the gains of the propertied bourgeoisie. The Code became an instrument of French rule in Europe and an object of emulation all over the globe. Together with the system of secular secondary education put in place by Bonaparte, it also became an important foundation stone of national unification.

NAPOLÉON'S PERSONAL CONTRIBUTION TO CODE

Bonaparte himself was only sporadically involved in the discussions on the draft Civil Code, which he initiated in 1800. He chose his legal experts carefully, and with an eye to the spirit of reconciliation which was the hallmark of his most creative reforms. One of them was [François-Denis] Tronchet, the lawyer who had defended Louis XVI before the National Convention. Like his colleague, [Felix] Bigot de Préameneu, he represented the common law tradition of northern France. They were joined by two ex-*parlementaires* from the Midi, Maleville, from Bordeaux, and Portalis from Aix, who had presided over the Council of the Ancients during the Directory period, before being deported after the left-wing coup of Fructidor Year 5. Portalis was nearly blind, but he had a phenomenal memory and an unparalleled knowledge of the law.

When the outline of the Civil Code was under examination by the Council of State, Bonaparte presided personally over about half of the meetings, intervening especially when the legal rights of women were under review. Was the Civil Code influenced by Bonaparte's own experience of marriage to an unfaithful and probably infertile wife? It is impossible to judge. He certainly used his influence to defend patriarchal values in the family law provisions, enhancing the authority of the *paterfamilias* and reducing the rights of illegitimate children. His energetic supervision was chiefly responsible for the lightning speed at which a few guiding principles were effectively transformed into a complete code of civil law, remarkable for its brevity, compactness and accessibility (it could be carried in a convenient pocket-sized volume). The first draft was finished in 1801, but in the Tribunate the Republican opposition rejected parts of the Civil Code which were found to be not revolutionary enough in spirit. But

Bonaparte eliminated this opposition by purging the Tribunate in 1802. The Civil Code was promulgated in 1804.

The Revolution had introduced new decrees, about 15,000 of them, which dramatically altered existing law. It freed property of all feudal burdens, for example, it introduced divorce and changed the rights of testators. It abolished seigneurial justice [justice administered by a noble or feudal lord] altogether. Revolutionary law was likely to change as rapidly as the republican régime itself, leaving a mass of edicts which were not always consistent with each other. The purpose of the Civil Code was to make order out of these confused legacies of the past. It was to give France, and then Europe, a social charter which would combine Ancien Régime custom with revolutionary innovations. In so doing, the Civil Code ratified the irrevocable end of seigneurialism and feudal privilege. The same laws would now apply equally to all citizens, whatever their social status. Unlike the legal patchwork of Ancien Régime France, the Civil Code would also apply nationally, in every corner of the Republic without exception.

Local custom, interacting with Roman, feudal and then revolutionary law made France a country of great juridical diversity. In the eighteenth century, [French political philosopher Baron de] Montesquieu had seen local diversity and provincial power as essential protection against the encroachments of a centralising monarchy. The monarchy, on the other hand, and then the eighteenth century Enlightenment, had long dreamed of the kind of legal uniformity which Bonaparte was to create, giving all subjects equal rights and duties under laws which were universal, rational and secular.

Regional differences were particularly marked in the law of inheritance. In the Midi, this tended to favour the eldest son at the expense of other children (the principle of primogeniture), in order to preserve the family estate intact. Northern customs, in contrast, were inclined to be more egalitarian in their treatment of descendants. Given provincial diversity, however, it is rash to generalise even this far: even in parts of the north, such as Flanders, complete equality of all descendants was not recognised by custom, since all heirs were considered equal only after the exclusion of offspring already provided with dowries. The Revolution's attempt to abolish feudal primogeniture and make complete equality between heirs compulsory came into conflict with habits deeply ingrained in half of France. In the Midi, too, there was a strong dowry system which southern lawyers did not want to abandon.

There was agreement on the fundamental principles of the Civil Code, which confirmed a decisive break with the pre-revolutionary world. The abolition of privilege, equality before the law, and the notion of careers open to talent were enshrined in this and every subsequent legal code designed for a democratic society. In preventing any return to the Ancien Régime in these areas, Napoléonic law developed the legacy of the liberal revolutionaries of 1789-91. The gains of the revolutionary bourgeoisie were preserved, since individual property rights were recognised within limits defined by the state. The unregulated economic liberalism of the Code also gave employers distinct advantages over their workers. Finally, the Civil Code demonstrated the secularisation of the law, most vividly illustrated by the Revolution's introduction of civil marriage and divorce. These ideas and their implications can be briefly examined in the fields of property law, inheritance law, and in the Code's interpretation of marriage and divorce.

The Civil Code embodied the modern conception of property ownership. It began with the premise that the individual had absolute rights of ownership. In practice, of course, the right to dispose of one's property was to be limited by inheritance law. Article 544 still stands today, defining property as "the right to enjoy and to dispose of one's property in the most absolute fashion, provided that it is not used in a manner prohibited by law." New legal constraints have from time to time eroded the absolute nature of individual property ownership: for example, in the form of laws which today protect the rights of tenants and control rents.

Property was seen as landed property, rather than commercial or industrial wealth—an assumption which, as we have seen, reflected the agricultural basis of the national economy at this time. In a spirit of bourgeois individualism, land was freed of feudal obligations and ancient servitudes. The principles of the Code were those suited to a mainly pre-industrial society of peasant and bourgeois landowners. Those principles, however, basic to a liberal and capitalist society, remain intact.

FAMILY LAW

The Code's provisions in the field of family law were conservative in the sense that the authority of fathers and husbands was strengthened. Fathers had the right to imprison their children for a month up to the age of 16, and for six months thereafter, and they controlled all their children's property until they reached the age of 18. A father could veto his son's marriage until he was 26, and his daughter's until she was 21. Even after the age of 25, "children" needed to obtain the formal advice of their parents before marrying. The husband could also administer the couple's joint property. Marriage itself, previously considered only as a sacrament, was completely secularised. The Revolution had abolished church courts and made marriage illegal unless a civil ceremony took place.

Dowry customs were a legal nightmare. In some areas of France, the couple's property was held in common; in others, any property brought to the marriage as a dowry remained the wife's property. The Civil Code solved the problem by allowing couples to decide on whichever arrangement they preferred in their marriage contract. In this area at least, the Code recognised the diversity of customary law while upholding patriarchal authority.

Patriarchy was not to have things all its own way. Individual children could not be disinherited, and children born outside the marriage could not inherit unless they had been officially legitimised. (This provision was a reversal of revolutionary law, which had given bastards full rights as heirs.) The Revolution had also tried to regulate the testator's freedom, by compelling him or her to give the heirs equal shares of the inheritance. This measure reflected the Revolution's new recognition of individual rights, which here overshadowed the rights of the family as a collective unit anxious to avoid a partition of its assets. The Civil Code was more moderate, seeking an equilibrium between the family and the individual, and between different practices in various parts of France: it allowed the testator to dispose of a quarter of the estate as he or she pleased (or more than a quarter, if there were fewer than three children), leaving the rest to be shared equally between heirs. A surviving spouse, however, had no automatic right to receive any portion of the estate. This régime recognised the egalitarianism of customary law, but still left some room to promote a principal heir, the favoured strategy of many peasant families.

The idea of equal shares for inheritors had important repercussions, which opponents of the Civil Code were not slow to point out. Some feared that it would lead to the excessive fragmentation of rural properties, reinforcing existing trends towards a society of small but struggling peasant proprietors. By the late nineteenth century, conservatives alleged that peasant families had responded by limiting the number of their offspring, to reduce fragmentation of the estate. A "natalist" argument emerged, accusing the Civil Code of contributing to the depopulation of the country.

DIVORCE LAWS

The laws on divorce provide an excellent example of the revolutionary attempt to secularise marriage and protect the rights of the individual. They illustrate, too, the direction of the Bonapartist compromise between the old and the revolutionary. The fight to divorce was preserved in the Civil Code, but Bonapartist policy was socially conservative and it explicitly recognised the "supremacy of the husband" as part of the "natural order."

In the Ancien Régime, divorce had been completely illegal. Although spouses had been allowed to apply to the courts for a judicial separation, this was expensive and rarely successful. In 1792 the French Revolution introduced the most liberal divorce provisions anywhere in the world, making divorce relatively easy, inexpensive and moreover, equally available to both men and women. The Civil Code repealed the remarkable legislation of 1792 but continued to allow divorce on more restricted grounds. The moderation of the Napoléonic divorce laws was clearly retrograde in comparison with the régime of 1792 and damaging to the status of women; but it should also be seen in the light of subsequent events. In 1816, the Bourbon Restoration abolished divorce altogether. Divorce was not legal again in France until the Naquet Law of 1884 revived the Napoléonic legislation.

The most startling innovation of the 1792 law was to allow divorce by mutual consent. In addition, divorce could be requested unilaterally on grounds of incompatibility, and also for other specified reasons. These included insanity, cruelty, desertion and emigration, criminal conviction, absence without news for five years and "dissolute morals." The immediate result was a flood of applications for divorce by couples who wanted to regularise separations and legitimise existing *de facto* relationships. This rush to divorce has given rise to unfair accusations that the Revolution encouraged immorality and a cynical attitude towards marriage. Such comments deserve to be dismissed as mere clerical

Napoléon is shown marrying Joséphine. The Napoléonic Civil Code damaged the status of women by restricting the liberal divorce laws of the French Revolution.

propaganda, blind to the liberating effect of the revolutionary legislation. Even the constitutional Church had accepted
divorce, although it was not so generous about remarriage.
The introduction of divorce had simply opened up a tap
through which poured the frustrations and miseries of thousands of couples, some deprived of legal separation, others
cohabiting but forced to do so illegally.

In Paris, between 1792 and 1803, there was one divorce for
every four marriages. Abandonment, emigration or desertion
constituted the most frequently cited reasons for divorce under the 1792 law. In Rouen there were 953 divorces, or one
for every eight marriages—a relatively high number for a
provincial city. Twenty-four per cent of divorces in Rouen
during this period were on the grounds of mutual consent,
and women appear as the main beneficiaries of the new legislation. In divorce proceedings in both Rouen and Metz initiated by one or the other spouse, women petitioned for divorce two-and-a-half times more frequently than did men.

The Civil Code permitted divorce—and before very long
Napoléon himself was to divorce Joséphine—but it ended
the liberality of the previous régime. Although Napoléonic
legislation did not deny the right to divorce by mutual consent, it nevertheless made it much more difficult than in the
past. Both spouses were obliged to provide written consent
to their divorce from their parents, and this written parental
statement had to be submitted four times within a year before divorce could be decreed. Even then, a judge had to examine the chances of reconciliation. This was divorce by
consent of a sort—but it seems more accurately described as
divorce by *parental* consent.

The Civil Code permitted divorce on only three other
grounds: ill-treatment (*excès injures graves*), criminal conviction or adultery. "Ill-treatment" was a legal euphemism
for wife-beating, which was a common enough reason for
divorce petitions. Society tolerated a limited degree of domestic violence, seen as part of the husband's natural right
to administer "correction" to wayward spouses. But if the
neighbours were kept awake by domestic disputes, or if one
violent party resorted to a knife or a blunt instrument, the
neighbourhood would intervene to restore peace, chastise
the offender and shelter the victim. This was sometimes
necessary after a drinking session or a religious festival
(which might amount to the same thing). Insanity was no

longer a basis for divorce under the Civil Code; families were expected to care for their own in time of ill-health.

The law on adultery discriminated against the woman. A man could petition for divorce on the grounds of his wife's infidelity, but a woman could only petition for divorce on the grounds of her husband's infidelity if he had an adulterous relationship with another woman in the conjugal dwelling itself. Women convicted of adultery were also liable to a two-year prison sentence, which was not the case for men. The law thus applied a double standard to sexual conduct, apparently condoning extra-marital affairs involving the husband but withholding the same tolerance from the wife. In many ways the Civil Code was ahead of its time, but its misogyny was an exception.

It is no wonder that divorces were rarer during the Napoléonic Empire. In Lyon, the annual divorce rate fell from eighty-seven before the Civil Code to seven after 1805. In Rouen, the average rate of divorce between 1803 and 1816 fell to only six per year. Only 7 per cent of these were divorces by mutual consent. Roderick Phillips' study of Rouen divorcees in the revolutionary and Napoléonic period suggests that divorce was most likely to occur when the woman had married between the ages of 15 and 20, when the marriage was less than five years old, or when the couple was childless. In fact, custody arrangements seem rarely to have been contentious, which suggests that the fate of children, if there were any, was not regarded as an important issue.

Divorce was overwhelmingly an urban option. In the department of the Haute-Garonne, for example, the number of divorces diminished in direct proportion to distance from the city of Toulouse. The city provided a multitude of jobs and refuges for women fleeing an unsatisfactory marriage, which were not available in small rural communities. The main beneficiaries of divorce legislation were young working women of the cities, where wage-earning opportunities for women in workshops and factories gave them a small but independent income. In the countryside, perhaps, the impact of Catholic teaching was stronger, and the traditional family economy was not so readily undermined by independent female wage-earners. Participation in the job market, however exploitative and poorly paid, may be considered here as a factor in female emancipation. In Rouen, 69 per cent of men who divorced and 72 per cent of women were workers and artisans, many of them employed in the city's textile industry. Divorce did not involve expensive litigation and it was not a rich person's prerogative. It involved appearance at a family court, but it was genuinely available to the urban lower and lower middle classes.

WOMEN AND THE LAW

The legal status of women had therefore been dramatically improved by the French Revolution, but Bonapartist legislation put a brake on the advances achieved. Divorce was still possible, but the law conceived it rather as a punishment for misconduct (usually by the woman), rather than as the humane recognition of an irretrievable marital breakdown. The Revolution had recognised women's civil rights, as equal access to divorce clearly demonstrated. There was, however, no corresponding recognition of women's *political* rights. In practice, no one had stopped women taking part in revolutionary politics. They attended political clubs and even if they were segregated in a special gallery, this did not prevent them from intervening and participating vigorously in debates. Women played a leading role, too, in the food and grocery riots of the Revolution, although in these cases their militancy reflected their important domestic role as supervisers of household consumption. Women, however, were still denied a political existence. They were not permitted to vote, and this was never on the political agenda of the Revolution, let alone the Consulate and Empire.

Bonaparte's régime continued to exclude women from the sphere of politics and public affairs, and it also made explicit several of the legal disabilities affecting women. Under the Civil Code, the wife owed obedience to the husband and she could not enter any legal contract without his permission. As we have seen, her infidelity was penalised much more severely than her partner's. The husband controlled his wife's domicile and could legally evict her and her children. If she was unmarried, a woman could not even witness a legal document. Patriarchal authority, buttressed by assumptions about innate female frailty and lack of seriousness, was underlined.

The Civil Code was not the only effort at legal reform made in this period. A Commercial Code was introduced in 1807, and in 1808 the Code of Criminal Procedure confirmed the principle of trial by jury.

The Penal Code of 1810 was conceived in a spirit of utilitarianism, valuing public order above the need for retribution against the criminal. Nevertheless, it contained some clauses reminiscent of the harshness of the Ancien Régime. The death penalty was retained for murder, arson and forgery. Parricide could be punished by amputation of the offending hand, and some criminals were still liable to be sentenced to forced labour for life (*peines perpétuelles*). Judges had more scope for leniency than the Constituent Assembly of 1791 had given them: they could use their discretion to award prison sentences whose length varied within a statutory range (for example, one to five years for theft).

THE INFLUENCE OF THE CODES ON EUROPE

The Napoléonic Codes, especially the Civil Code, had a European and even global significance. The Code was an integral part of the spread of French Revolutionary ideas all over the world. It became an instrument of French conquest and a weapon in the war against the coalition. It promised to liberate Europe from clericalism and feudalism. It was introduced in Belgium and the Netherlands, the Rhineland, Bavaria, Switzerland and parts of Italy. The Code helped to win the support of the local bourgeoisie for French rule. Its influence in these areas of Europe is still present today. It was translated for the benefit of the Spanish and Portuguese, and it inspired law codes in Egypt and South America, Louisiana, Japan, Rumania and Yugoslavia.

The Civil Code inspired European intellectuals: in Dresden, the playwright [Heinrich von] Kleist had a burning ambition to translate it into German. At the same time, it antagonised conservatives. It was accused of peddling philosophical abstraction, and of spreading the dogma of individualism which would dissolve the social fabric of the European Ancien Régime. Above all, it upheld divorce, and threatened to destroy the family, a sacred institution and one which was fundamental to social stability. This is perhaps what [British foreign secretary Viscount] Castlereagh [who guided the Grand Alliance against Napoléon] meant, when he is reported to have remarked at the Congress of Vienna: "There is no point in destroying France, the Civil Code will do it for us."

In France itself, the Civil Code has had a long life. It has survived the upheavals and many changes of constitution which punctuated French history in the following century and a half. As a result, it has been claimed that the Civil Code itself should be considered the "real" Constitution of France. The Codes have been adapted to recognise new ideas, such as modern notions of equality between men and women, but their basic structure is still intact. The Code was an instrument in the spread of revolutionary ideas; it preserved the essential social gains of the Revolution, abolishing privilege, recognising equality and individualism, and completely extracting the legal system from its old religious framework. By reconciling different legal traditions within France, and striking a compromise between a wide variety of regional customs, the Code helped to establish a unified nation. It endured because it was a body of secular law which applied to all citizens without exemption, no matter where in France they lived.

A Revolution in Education

Will and Ariel Durant

The husband-and-wife team of Will Durant and Ariel Durant are internationally renowned historians and authors of the multi-volume *The Story of Civilization*. The following reading is from volume eleven, *The Age of Napoléon*. In this excerpt, the Durants discuss Napoléon's complete reconstruction of France's educational system under a more centralized and military-like structure. They explain that the emperor's main motivations were to use education to establish social peace by teaching a devotion to law and order—and to control the political and moral opinions of the students. Toward this end, Napoléon established the Imperial University, which would be solely responsible for providing teachers for all the secondary schools (lycées) in France. The Durants conclude that, despite his distaste for intellectuals, Napoléon reorganized and supported the entire university system to such an extent that France remained at the forefront of scientific and scholastic achievement in Europe for the next fifty years.

Napoléon, during his Consulate, [tried] to give a new order and stability to postrevolutionary France by a Code of Civil Law, and a Concordat of peace and cooperation between his government and the traditional religion of the people. To these formative forces he proposed to add a third by reorganizing the educational system of France. [According to Napoléon], "Of all social engines, the school is probably the most efficacious, for it exercises three kinds of influence on the young lives it enfolds and directs: one through the master, another through con-discipleship, and the last

Reprinted with permission of Simon & Schuster from *The Story of Civilization*, vol. 11: *The Age of Napoléon*, by Will and Ariel Durant. Copyright © 1975 by Will and Ariel Durant.

through rules and regulations." He was convinced that one reason for the breakdown of law and order during the Revolution was its inability to establish, amid the life-and-death conflicts of the time, a system of education adequately replacing that which the Church had previously maintained. Splendid plans had been formulated, but neither money nor time could be spared to realize them; primary education had been left to priests and nuns, or to lay schoolmasters maintained just above starvation by parents or communes; secondary education had barely survived in lycées dispensing courses in science and history, with scant attention to the formation of character. Napoléon thought of public education in political terms: its function was to produce intelligent but obedient citizens. "In establishing a corps of teachers," he said, with a candor unusual in governments, "my principal aim is to secure the means for directing political and moral opinions. . . . So long as one grows up without knowing whether to be republican or monarchist, Catholic or irreligious, the state will never form a nation; it will rest on vague and uncertain foundations; it will be constantly exposed to disorder and change."

Having restored the Church to association with the government, he allowed semimonastic organizations, like the Frères des Écoles Chrétiennes, to attend to primary instruction, and nuns to teach well-to-do girls; but he refused to let the Jesuits reenter France. Nevertheless, he admired them for their strict organization as a dedicated guild of teachers. "The essential thing," he wrote (February 16, 1805), "is a teaching body like that of the Jesuits of old." "While I was with him," [Napoléon's secretary for dictation, Louis] Bourrienne recalled, "he often told me that it was necessary that all schools, colleges, and other establishments for public instruction be subject to military discipline." In a note of 1805 Napoléon proposed that "a teaching order could be formed if all the managers, directors, and professors in the Empire were under one or more chiefs, like the generals, provincials, etc., of the Jesuits," and if it were the rule that no one could fill a higher position in the organization unless he had passed through various lower stages. It would be desirable, too, that the teacher not marry, or that he defer marriage "till he has secured an adequate position and income . . . to support a family."

THE ESTABLISHMENT OF THE IMPERIAL UNIVERSITY

A year later (May 10, 1806) Antoine-François de Fourcroy, director general of public instruction, secured from the Corps Législatif [the French Legislature] a provisional decree that "there shall be established, under the name of the Imperial University, a body exclusively charged with the work of teaching throughout the Empire." (The University of Paris, founded *c.* 1150, had been suppressed by the Revolution in 1790.) This new university was to be not merely a union of various faculties—theology, law, medicine, science, and literature; it was to be the sole producer of teachers for the secondary schools of France, and was to include all its living and teaching graduates. These "lycées" were to be established in one or more cities of each *département,* with a curriculum combining the classic languages and literatures with the sciences; they were to be financed by the municipality, but all their teachers were to be graduates of the university; and no one was to be promoted to a higher post unless he had previously held those below it, and had obeyed his superiors like a soldier obeying an officer. To persuade French youths to enter this treadmill, Napoléon provided 6,400 scholarships, whose recipients pledged themselves to the teaching profession and promised to defer marriage at least to the age of twenty-five. As their final reward [Napoléon said] they were to "have clearly before them the prospect of rising to the highest offices of the state." "All this," Napoléon told Fourcroy, "is only a commencement; by and by we shall do more, and better."

He did better, from his point of view, by restoring (1810), as a branch of the university, the École Normale, where select students, living in common under military discipline, were given special training by a prestigious faculty. . . . By 1813 all college teachers were expected to be graduates of the École Normale; science began to prevail over the classics in the college curriculum, and set the intellectual tone of educated France. The École Polytechnique, established during the Revolution, was changed into a military academy, where the physical sciences became the servants of war. Several provincial universities survived the Emperor's martial sweep, and private colleges were allowed to operate under license and periodical examination by the university. As the authoritarian mood relaxed, individual lecturers were permitted to use university halls to give special courses, and students were allowed to take these as they chose.

FRANCE'S LEADING INTELLECTUAL INSTITUTE

At the top of the intellectual pyramid was the Institut National de France. The French Academy, suppressed in 1793, had been restored in 1795 as Class II of the new Institute. Napoléon was proud of his membership in the Institute, but when its moral and political section, in 1801, presumed to discourse on how a government should be run, he ordered [French general] Comte Louis-Philippe de Ségur to "tell the Second Class of the Institute that I will have no political subjects treated at its meetings." The Institute then contained many old rebels faithful to the Enlightenment and the Revolution, who privately laughed or wept at the official restoration of the Catholic Church. [French philosopher] Cabanis and [French philosopher and soldier Antoine] Destutt de Tracy had used the word *ideology* as the study of the formation of ideas; Napoléon called these psychologists and philosophers "ideologues" as men too immersed in ideas, and reveling in reason, to perceive and understand the realities of life and history. These intellectuals, spreading their notions through countless publications, were, in his judgment, obstacles to good government. "The men who write well and are eloquent," he said, "have no solidity of judgment." He cautioned his brother Joseph, then (July 18, 1807) ruling Naples: "You live too much with literary people." As for the intellectuals who were buzzing in the salons, "I regard scholars and wits the same as coquettish women; one should frequent them and talk with them, but never choose one's wife from among such women, or one's ministers from among such men."

On January 23, 1803, he reorganized the Institute into four classes, omitting the moral and political category. Class I, which he valued most, was to study the sciences. . . . Class II had forty members, devoted to the language and literature of France; it replaced the old French Academy, and resumed work on the *Dictionnaire*. . . . Class III, with forty members, dealt with ancient and Oriental history, literature, and art. . . . Class IV—the Académie des Beaux-Arts—included ten painters, six sculptors, six architects, three engravers, and three composers. . . .

Aside from his distaste for ideologues, Napoléon supported the Institute heartily, eager to make it an embellishment of his reign. Every member of the Institute received from the government an annual salary of fifteen hundred francs; each permanent secretary of a class received six thousand. In February and March each class presented to the Emperor a report of the work done in its department. Napoléon was pleased with the total picture, for ([Napoléon's secretary Claude-François] Méneval claimed) "this general review of literature, science, and art . . . showed that human intelligence, far from going back, did not halt in its constant march toward progress." We may question the "constant," but there is no doubt that the reorganization of science and scholarship under Napoléon placed their practitioners at the head of the European intellect for half a century.

The Concordat

Geoffrey Ellis

Despite the fact that the vast majority of French people were Catholic, the French Revolution instituted an aggressive policy of destroying the considerable influence of the Catholic Church in French politics. Although Napoléon inherited this tumultuous schism, he promptly set about reconciling with the Church through a treaty with Pope Pius VII. Even though this agreement, known as the Concordat, was tremendously popular among the people, Geoffrey Ellis maintains that many hard-liners saw it as a betrayal of the principles of the French Revolution. However, Ellis argues that the Concordat with the pope in 1801 was not an act of faith on Napoléon's part, but rather a calculated step to use religion to increase his own power within France as well as the rest of Europe. Ellis is the author of *The Napoléonic Empire* and *Napoléon*, from which this essay is excerpted.

Napoléon's Concordat with the pope in 1801 has often been seen as one of his more conciliatory and popular acts during the early Consulate. Just how popular that agreement was can be gauged only in relation to the deep crisis which had engulfed the French Church since the conflict over the Civil Constitution of the Clergy (July 1790). That reform, with its new provisions for higher and more regular salaries for parish priests, would perhaps have been welcome to most of them, *de facto*. But the requirement of an oath to the Civil Constitution (November 1790) had soon confronted them with a major crisis of conscience, especially once Pius VI had outlawed the measure and instructed the French clergy to refuse the oath in March and April 1791. All but seven bishops had obeyed the pope, while the lesser clergy as a whole had divided roughly evenly on the issue, although the incidence of non-jurorship [refusal to take the oath] was very high in several departments.

Many of the refractory clergy had thereafter joined forces with royalists in the counter-revolutionary movement, again chiefly in the western provinces.

A SPLIT CHURCH

One of the Revolution's legacies to Napoléon was thus a schismatic Church and total alienation from Rome, and the problem had been exacerbated by successive regimes in various ways. Appalled by the excesses of the 'dechristianization' campaign launched by Jacobin militants in 1793–94, the Montagnard government [noted for their democratic outlook] had turned against and eventually eliminated its main perpetrators, but without placating the millions of Catholic faithful. The Thermidorian regime [the moderate leaders who overthrew the harsh rule of Maximilien de Robespierre], for its part, had in effect admitted its inability to establish the constitutional church when, on 21 February 1795, it proclaimed 'the liberty of cults' and at the same time refused State subsidies to any of them. While maintaining the same official neutrality, the Directory had nevertheless asserted its secular republican principles in a new wave of repressive measures against non-jurors in 1798.

In spite of this confused and uneasy backdrop, it now seems that the refractory church had come through the years of the Directory spiritually and in some ways materially stronger than the rump of the constitutional church. Although estimates vary, it is likely that a few thousand of its clergy had perished at the hands of revolutionaries and many more had been driven into exile, while its buildings had frequently been ransacked for precious metals and other useful materials. Yet a large number of non-juror priests had somehow managed to survive those troubles without physical mishap or prolonged exile, finding food and shelter in clandestine retreats, usually among rural communities, which they continued to serve through the old Catholic rites. Thus encouraged, the response of the Catholic laity had also become stronger and more open. Olwen Hufton, in a fascinating study of the question during the years 1796–1801, its time of greatest obscurity in texts published hitherto, shows that there was then not only a religious but indeed a clerical revival in many regions where Catholicism had deep roots. It was (so to speak) 'unofficial', it was also more pronounced among French women than their menfolk, and it worked in favour of the refractory clergy almost entirely. All this, Hufton argues, 'is the story of religious survival and of how a church was reestablished from below long before the Concordat, which merely restored and placed a hierarchy on a legal footing, made peace with Rome and allowed the people to commit their spiritual well-being into professional hands'.

Now, while it may be going rather too far to say that the Concordat merely recognized a *fait accompli*, as Hufton claims in the same place, there is no doubt that Napoléon had an acute sense of this growing religious mood among Catholic communities. Pius VI had died in French hands at Valence in August 1799, and the election in March 1800 of a new pope, Cardinal Chiaramonti, a Benedictine monk and archbishop of Imola, who assumed the name Pius VII, offered the first consul a favourable opportunity for reconciliation with Rome. It is well known that his motives were not spiritual but pragmatic. 'In religion,' as he once famously remarked, 'I see not the mystery of the Incarnation, but the mystery of the social order.' He was also keen to secure papal recognition of his coup, which he reckoned would help him to pacify the Vendée, detach the émigrés from the cause of the exiled Bourbons, and facilitate the assimilation of annexed or occupied areas like Belgium, the Rhenish left bank and Piedmont, all strongly Catholic.

OVERTURES OF PEACE WITH THE CHURCH

As soon as he was free from the military commitments of the victorious Marengo campaign of 1800, Napoléon made his first overtures to Rome. Pius VII could see obvious advantages for the Church in an agreement, but his initial reaction was nevertheless both suspicious and cautious. It was his fear of a French occupation of the Papal States which chiefly persuaded him in September that year to send [Cardinal Guiseppe] Spina and [monk] Caselli as special plenipotentiaries to Paris. Napoléon was represented at first by the abbé Bernier, who as a former Chouan [French rebels who revolted against Napoléon] seemed a shrewd choice, and at the same time [Maurice, Count] d'Hauterive, one of [Napoléon's foreign minister Charles de] Talleyrand's collaborators, was instructed to draw up the project of a Concordat. This, however, was only the start of what proved to be a difficult, laborious, and prolonged process of secret negotiation. As his impatience grew, Napoléon decided to take advantage of his peace with Austria at Lunéville (9 February 1801), which strengthened his position in Italy and obliged the pope to be more pliant, by adopting rougher tactics. He sent [Alexis] Cacault, a diplomatic agent, to put direct pressure on Pius in Rome, and in May 1801 delivered a virtual ultimatum to him. But still there was no real progress, and when Cacault was recalled, the pope thought it best to send his secretary of state, Cardinal [Ercole] Consalvi, to Paris in an attempt to avoid a total rupture. Even then, in spite of Napoléon's repeated insistence on a prompt agreement, none was forthcoming until [Etienne] Bernier, Joseph Bonaparte, and [Emmanuel] Crétet (for the French Republic) and Consalvi and Spina (for the papacy) finally signed the Concordat at 2 a.m. on 16 July 1801. It was ratified in Rome on 15 August and in Paris on 10 September that year.

In view of its long and troubled gestation, the Concordat was a surprisingly brief document. Its terms, as originally agreed, and in spite of some deliberate vagueness, gave the first impression of a reasonable enough compromise on both sides. Napoléon did not want an official religion of state nor an established Church with exclusive constitutional privileges. Instead, he recognized that Roman Catholicism was 'the religion of the vast majority of French citizens'. As such, it was to be freely and openly practised in France, in conformity with police regulations considered necessary for public tranquillity. Pius VII, for his part, formally recognized the legitimacy of the Consular Republic. The French dioceses were to be reorganized with the agreement of both contracting parties, and incumbent bishops would if necessary be required to resign, pending their renomination or the appointment of new ones. The first consul was to make all nominations to archbishoprics and bishoprics, while the pope's right of canonical investiture was recognized in return. A new oath of loyalty to the Consular government would be required of all bishops and lower clergy. The bishops were to make a new delimitation of the parishes of their dioceses, but it could not take effect without the government's consent. The appointment of the parish clergy, now also entrusted to the bishops, similarly had to meet with the government's approval. Bishops might establish a cathedral chapter and a seminary in their dioceses, but with no guarantee of State subsidies. 'A suitable salary' for bishops and parish priests would, however, be guaranteed by the government.

The Concordat also included important statements on the Revolutionary land settlement, and these need particular attention, since they affected a large number of French citizens. The rather vague terms of article 12, which put at the bishops' disposal all metropolitan churches, cathedrals, parish and other churches not yet alienated and which were 'necessary for worship', almost invited disputes over their proper definition. By the far more crucial article 13, and in terms which left no such doubt, the pope gave a solemn undertaking that neither he nor his successors would disturb in any way those who had acquired alienated Church lands and now enjoyed the revenues attached to them, and that the proprietary rights of their heirs would be similarly respected.

THE ORGANIC ARTICLES CHANGE THE AGREEMENT

We can only surmise how the Concordat might have worked if its original terms had been duly honoured in its implementation. It was not in fact formally published in Paris until Easter Sunday (8 April) 1802, seven months after its ratification. In the meantime Napoléon had established a general directory of cults within the ministry of the interior on 7 October 1801 and appointed Portalis, a councillor of state, as its head. Much more provocatively, he had also had a whole series of so-called 'Organic Articles' drawn up, and these were simply added to the Concordat unilaterally and published at the same time. So far from giving his prior approval to them, Pius VII had not even been consulted on their details, and he was understandably offended by them. Not least, they complicated the position of his special legate to Paris, Cardinal Caprara, from the start.

The Organic Articles, a detailed code of seventy-seven articles in fact, greatly restrained the rights and powers the pope believed he had been given in the preceding July, and at the same time subjected the whole ecclesiastical establishment to much stricter control by the government. They amounted, in effect, to a comprehensive reformulation of caesaro-papist principles. By such measures, Napoléon clearly reaffirmed and extended the old 'Gallican Liberties' of the French Church, now under the auspices of the secular state, and signalled his determination to hold all forms of ultramontanism [advocating supreme papal authority in matters of faith] in check. On this basis, then, the Concordat was implemented in France. The ecclesiastical hierarchy of archbishops, bishops, parish priests (*curés*), vicars, and sub-ordinates (*desservants*) was indeed reconstituted, but it was now grafted into the administrative structures of the civil state, and in diminished form at that. France was divided into 10 archbishoprics, 60 bishoprics, and only about 3,000 parishes whose area roughly corresponded to that of the cantons. Strict conditions were laid down for the nomination

THE POPE FORGIVES NAPOLÉON

Despite Napoléon's long embattled history with Pius VII—which included breaking the Concordat, followed by persecuting and imprisoning the pope—Pius VII came to Napoléon's defense when he was imprisoned on St. Helena. In the following excerpt, the pope instructs Cardinal Ercole Consalvi to petition the allies to improve Napoléon's living conditions on St. Helena.

Napoléon's family . . . have made known to Us through Cardinal Fesch that the craggy island of Saint Helena is mortally injurious to health, and that the poor exile is dying by inches. We have been deeply grieved to hear this, as without doubt you will be, for We ought both to remember that, after God, it is to him chiefly that is due the re-establishment of religion in the great kingdom of France. The pious and courageous initiative of 1801 [the Concordat] has made Us long forget and pardon the wrongs that followed. Savona and Fontainebleau were only mistakes due to temper, or the frenzies of human ambition. [Pius was imprisoned in Savona, Italy, and Fountainbleau, France, by Napoléon, between 1809–1813, until he agreed to sign the Concordat.] The concordat was a healing act, Christian and heroic. Napoléon's mother and family have appealed to Our pity and Our generosity; We think it right to respond to that appeal. We are certain that We shall only be ordering you to act as you would wish to act when We instruct you to write on Our behalf to the allied sovereigns, and in particular to the Prince Regent [the future George IV of England]. He is your dear and good friend, and We wish you to ask him to lighten the sufferings of so hard an exile. Nothing would give Us greater joy than to have contributed to the lessening of Napoléon's hardships. He can no longer be a danger to anybody. We would not wish him to become a cause for remorse.

E.E.Y. Hales, *The Emperor and the Pope: The Story of Napoléon and Pius VII.* Garden City, NY: Doubleday, 1961.

to bishoprics of Frenchmen only, aged at least thirty years, and non-residence was specifically outlawed.

As first consul, and then emperor, Napoléon also assumed authority over a whole range of internal ecclesiastical business. It is worth noting here that the Church's former role in the registration of births, deaths, marriages, and other vital statistics had already been taken over by the civil state during the 1790s. This might be seen as a largely administrative process, following logically from the various Revolutionary policies aimed at secularizing the government of France and reducing clerical influence in public life. Napoléon not only maintained that system but went much further. He claimed the right to intercept and inspect papal communications with France, and even to interfere in the training of its clergy. The deliberately vague police regulations to which the French Church was subject gave an ominous foretaste of things to come, and they not surprisingly alarmed the pope from the earliest days.

The Organic Articles provided for the payment of clerical salaries, though not of the maintenance costs of church fabrics, by the State. Here again, the element of hierarchy was quite conspicuous. An archbishop was to receive 15,000 francs a year, a bishop 10,000, and a parish priest 1,000 or 1,500, depending on his station. In practice, however, there was very little financial security for most of the lower clergy. Under the Organic Articles, only the *curés* appointed to the chief towns of cantons were assured of tenure. All the rest, about four-fifths of the parish clergy, were considered removable and were to serve in subsidiary stations (*succursales*) at the bishops' pleasure. In this way, from top to bottom, the concordatory clergy in effect became either fully salaried officials or provisional servants of the State. On an analogy with their civil homologues, the bishops have been likened to 'prefects in purple' and the tenured priests to 'mayors in black'. Clerical careerism, which the Revolution had done much to destroy, could revive only with the government's approval. . . .

A NEW POLICY TOWARD JEWS AND PROTESTANTS

It is clear that Napoléon regarded the Concordat in its published form as a part, albeit much the most important part, of a more general reorganization of the religious life of his subjects. Officially at least, the Civil Code of 1804 was to grant religious freedom to all of them. There were in France at that time around 480,000 Calvinists and 200,000 Lutherans. Having promulgated Organic Articles for the public regulation of these Protestant communities in April 1802, Napoléon decided that the State would assume responsibility for the salaries of their pastors as from 1804. He was unwilling to extend this last provision to the much less numerous Jewish communities, but by a series of measures issued in 1806 he assimilated their newly formed consistories into his religious organization, once again under centralized control, and then established the Grand Sanhedrin of European rabbis in 1807. Even so, the civic status of the Jews under Napoléon was rather more ambivalent than they might have hoped for after their notional emancipation by the Revolutionary laws of 1790 and 1791, which in fact had never been fully honoured. French Protestants, by contrast, were free to take a much more active part in the public life of the Consulate and Empire, especially in areas of the south and east where their population was relatively dense, and their traditional foothold in banking and trade also remained firm.

In all, Napoléon clearly conducted his religious policy as an integral function of his executive authority. Although deeply concerned by the terms of the Organic Articles and the manner of their publication, Pius VII thought it best to steer clear of a major quarrel over their implementation in the early years. He accepted the nomination of Joseph Fesch, Napoléon's uncle, as archbishop of Lyons, and even made him a cardinal in 1803. After much initial hesitation, not helped by Fesch's ineptitude during a brief term as ambassador to Rome in 1804, the pope finally agreed to travel to Paris for the Imperial coronation in December that year. But the public presentation of Church–State relations as a masterstroke of Napoléonic statesmanship could not be continued indefinitely. Those relations worsened steadily from 1805.

Napoléon's Political Use of Theater

Michael Polowetzky

French theater was extremely popular during
Napoléon's rule, partly because the largely illiterate
population could enjoy the entertainment. Although
many plays were simple melodramatic entertain-
ments, some were also political in content, attacking
social and religious conventions or satirizing public
policies. Fearful of the influence of such works on
public opinion, Napoléon mounted an aggressive
campaign to monitor and manipulate French theater.
In the following excerpt from *A Bond Never Broken:
The Relations Between Napoléon and the Authors of
France,* author Michael Polowetzky describes
Napoléon's detailed campaign to control which plays
were produced, how they were written, and even how
the actors performed them. But Napoléon's interest in
theater went beyond merely the content of the plays;
he also sent his spies to mingle among the audiences
to gauge public attitudes toward the government.

The First Consul [Napoléon] now held absolute political
domination over France. But he soon discovered that this did
not mean he had the same control over his nation's culture,
especially its literature. While Napoléon's political rivals
may have been easy to master, literature was to prove a
much more formidable opponent. And of all literature's
components, the theater was to be among his primary concerns throughout his years in power.

Much of Napoléon's early life is shrouded in mystery.
However, one fact is clear: he was interested in the theater
from a very early age. When he first arrived at the boarding
school at Autun from Corsica at the age of ten in 1779,
Napoléon was introduced to the theater of classical Greece

Excerpted from *A Bond Never Broken: The Relations Between Napoléon and the Authors of France,* by Michael Polowetzky (Rutherford, NJ: Fairleigh Dickinson University Press, 1993). Copyright © Associated University Presses, 1993. Reprinted by permission of Associated University Presses.

and Rome. Later at the military academy of Brienne, after he had gained a command of French, the young cadet studied the drama of his adopted country. His favorite dramatic style was tragedy. He liked tragedy as depicted by the ancients, whose works he usually read in French translation, but most of all, he admired it in the neoclassical tradition of the seventeenth century, as depicted in the works of Jean Racine and Pierre Corneille. For Napoléon, these plays portrayed all that was noble in Man. Their influence, he believed, could create a society where individuals lived by, even died for, high ideals. "Great tragedy," Napoléon remarked later on St. Helena, "is the school of great men." Alas, this style of drama, which was so closely associated with the Ancien Régime, fell into disrepute with the coming of the Revolution. Obviously, Napoléon's attempts over the years to restore the seventeenth-century neoclassical theater to popularity along with all its connections to Versailles and the Sun King were partly motivated by the desire to build up the prestige of his new regime. But at the same time, however, Napoléon had a strong personal interest in drama that went beyond mere politics. It was this mixture of artistic appreciation and worldly ambitions that was to prove the motivating force in Napoléon's policy toward the literature of his day.

Drama was extremely popular when Napoléon came to power. Paris had more than thirty theaters of various sizes and genres. The Théatre de la Cité, for instance, presented mainly melodrama and seated two thousand people. There were fewer theaters in the provincial cities; Bordeaux, for example, had only four. But because of the existence of many amateur societies and traveling acting troupes, no part of France was unacquainted with dramatic literature. In some ways the theater of revolutionary France was similar to the Hollywood of the 1930s and 1940s. In a nation shaken by economic depression, unemployment, political turmoil, and war, the theater provided a place where one could go for a few hours and forget all one's troubles. "Happy," a Parisian once remarked, "is the person who attaches less importance to the depositions of the civil code than to the gestures of an actress." Also like Hollywood, the French theater was dominated by what was once called the star system. Just as the crowds of a later century clamored for a glimpse of Clark Gable or Greta Garbo, so people in 1799 would gawk at Talma and Mlle. Georges. . . .

However, the theater in 1799 was not entirely an escapist vehicle; other types of drama existed as well. Since ancient Athens, plays have contained political and social comment, and drama in revolutionary France was no exception. This could be seen in plays commonly called "piéces des circumstance." These were works written by authors who took such provocative pen names as "Brise-Tout." They were sarcastic, often bitter attacks on societal and religious conventions. *Gioruette*, for instance, made fun of the Holy Family's flight from Herod into Egypt. In 1799, the line that separated entertainment from outright political advocacy was getting ever narrower.

THEATER AS POPULARITY POLL

During his rule, few things escaped Napoléon's notice. Each day he received a report from the Paris police describing what the prefect judged to be the most important events of the day. Beginning sporadically in 1802 and then daily from 1804, Napoléon also received similar dispatches from Fouché concerning national affairs. After 1805, when Napoléon had overrun Western Germany, the various client states of the Confederation of the Rhine were required to send the Emperor such reports as well. These "bulletins," as most historians describe them today, were usually about a page or two long and were divided into several subjects. A bulletin might contain information on food prices, public gatherings, violent crimes, and visits by foreign dignitaries. Quite often bulletins also included information on the theater collected by undercover policemen who mingled with the audience. The number of bulletins dealing with "Spectacles" runs into the hundreds. On his own initiative, Napoléon wrote several hundred letters and official memoranda after 1800 that also dealt with various aspects of the stage.

Despite his involvement in the theater, Napoléon was not the first French leader since the Revolution to be concerned with its political implications. The Directory had been interested, too; its police had also reported on the stage. [Directory member and head of the Army of the Interior Paul] Barras had earlier banned plays that openly called for the overthrow of the regime. He also required that plays often open with the singing of patriotic songs. But the consulate's interest in dramatic art was more far reaching. It was on the stage, Napoléon and those around him believed, that the new regime might learn what was the thinking of the nation. "In politics," wrote Louis de Bonald, "all theory is false if it neglects to calculate the passions of men." Few statements are more true. So often in history, governments fall because they misunderstand the yearnings of the people. Had not the Bourbon monarchy been fatally weakened because it was unwilling or unable to perceive the gravity of the desire for change among the various classes? Did not [French Revolution leader Maximilien] Robespierre's continuation of the Reign of Terror after all immediate danger to the state had passed, eventually erode his support and lead to his downfall? Napoléon was quite aware of these facts. He had no intention of making the same mistakes as his predecessors.

But how could Napoléon analyze the moods and perceptions of the general population any better than those who had come before him? How could he grasp what today is called public opinion? He had established the Cabinet Noir—a division of the ministry of post—which secretly opened mail. [French Minister of Police Joseph] Fouché employed more than three hundred informants in social circles. One of them, Mme. de Genlis, sent him reports detailing the activities of intellectual dissidents like Mme. de Staël, along with influential figures in the middle and upper classes. Important information about popular opinion was also gleaned from the wealth of newspapers, books, pamphlets, and libelles.

NAPOLÉON SPIES ON THEATER PATRONS

Despite all these resources, the government's intelligence network actually supplied Napoléon with information on only a small percentage of the population. The vast majority of Frenchmen were peasants or working class for whom correspondence, newspapers, "subversive" books, and the literary salon meant nothing. Perhaps 57 percent of the Parisian working class was illiterate. In rural areas in the West, illiteracy was as high as 84 percent. Frequently, literacy at this time has been measured by the ability to sign one's name to a marriage contract or a will. But after birth, marriage and death were the main events in a working class person's life. Therefore, many of those who were able to scribble their names may never have felt a desire or need to learn anything further. Finally, while it is true that 30 percent of the Parisian working class owned books and could probably read fairly well, the vast majority of these books were bibles, psalters, and other purely religious material, signifying their owners had no interest or contact with the major literary movements of their time. Another important group the government had to keep its eye on was the criminal population. Although illiteracy was declining in this sector, 40 percent of those who lived outside the law were still unable to read. And among female criminals specifically, the degree of illiteracy was as high as 90 percent. Historians will argue forever whether the lower classes were active participants in the events of the Revolution or whether they were led by others. Be that as it may, the lower classes were an instrumental force in the Revolution, and their beliefs and aspirations had to be considered by Napoléon or anyone else who wished to be the leader of the nation. Given the government's current inability to measure the feelings of such a large part of the population, a new strategy had to be developed. The gauging of public opinion by polls was still a thing of the future, and probably would not have worked anyway. However, it is clear from the police bulletins and from Napoléon's own correspondence that he and his government had settled on their own way of detecting the feelings of the population as a whole—the stage.

Unlike today, the theater of 1799 was not patronized by a small percentage of the middle and upper classes. The theater was one of the few institutions in 1799 that was open to all sections of French society. The price for tickets, often as little as twelve sous, was cheap enough to be bought by an ordinary unskilled day laborer. Society ladies like Mme. Tallien dressed in lavish attire, sat cheek by jowl with women from the outer faubourgs whose garments had been passed down from mother to daughter. The melodramatic style that was then so popular was not profound and could be understood without any deep knowledge of literature. Finally, and most important, attendance at the theater did not require a high degree of literacy. All these factors, especially the last, assured that a large contingent of the uneducated classes was always in the audience. At the same time, the unfettering of dramatic free expression, coupled with the expansion of the audience to include the uneducated classes, provided opponents of the government with a new and often very effective means of spreading dissident ideas among them. The new regime appears to have been quite aware of the theater's potential as a political barometer and believed that audience reactions to stage dramas could at last be a tool to gauge lower class political opinion. If the government frequently misread the popular mood in this process, it also detected other feelings that were quite true.

The police began to carry out their new method of measuring public opinion almost from the beginning of the new regime. Their observations tell us not only about how the government interpreted public opinion, but also about its own desires and concerns. The bulletin for 14 Pluviôse (3 February) 1800, for instance, mentions a play staged at the Théatre de Vaudeville, one of the places that specialized in comedies. It was entitled *Guillaume ou le Voyageur* and was based loosely on the life of Guillaume de Malesherbes, the liberal monarchist who was a patron of the *Encyclopédie*, who aided Louis XVI in the reforms of the early years of his reign, and who died in the Reign of Terror. The police report indicates the play was highly acclaimed by the audience. During this early part of the Consulate while Napoléon's government was considering a rapprochement with the Right, it is not surprising these cheers were viewed as a sign of growing royalist sentiment. . . .

THEATER AS A POLITICAL TOOL

Police reports on the theater would continue to reach Napoléon throughout his years in power. However, he had no intention of remaining merely a passive observer. Napoléon not only wished to use the stage to measure public opinion, he also wanted to utilize it to shape public opinion. His attempt to do this began very early. A play judged subversive was banned only six days after Brumaire [the coup d'état of 18 Brumaire (1799) which overthrew the Directory and established Napoléon as the head of the French government]. Then on 27 Nivôse (17 January) 1800, the government ordered the reduction of the number of Paris theaters from thirty to thirteen in order that they could be better monitored by the police. The new constitution also provided no legal protection for the stage and left it entirely at the mercy of the state's pleasure.

But it was soon apparent that political opinions expressed in art, which a government finds objectionable, cannot be totally eliminated unless that regime is willing to silence art all together, something Napoléon's government did not want to do. Some authors always received better

treatment than others. Censors were not given set guide-
lines to follow; they also were not all of the same political
opinion nor of the same degree of perceptiveness. As a result, plays that contained or were suspected of containing
dissident opinions still managed to reach the stage, still
managed to reach wide audiences.

One example of this kind of play was *Eduard en Ecosse,*
first performed at the Théatre de la République on 29 Pluviôse (17 February) 1802. While set in Scotland at the time
of the Second Jacobite Rebellion in 1745, this drama by the
popular Alexandre Duval was clearly a heroic portrayal of
the émigrés during the Revolution. Since the signing of the
Concordat [a treaty between France and the papacy which
regulated the role of the Roman Catholic Church] with
Rome in 1802, large numbers of former émigrés had been
allowed to return from exile. The police report of that date
states that a considerable contingent of them had come to
the theater especially to see this play. At many points they
broke into loud cheers and tried to start a royalist demonstration. Napoléon, in fact, was in the audience. Although we
do not know his personal reaction to the episode, it is interesting that his presence did not intimidate his opponents in
the audience. . . .

PUNISHING THE POLITICALLY INCORRECT

Having realized that his original restraints were not enough
to control the stage, Napoléon now decided to wield a heavier hand. The toughest action he ever took was against Louis
Dupaty, another popular playwright of the day, after he produced a work called *L'Antichambre.* This was a farce which
involved three besotted flunkies in green livery. The cos-
tumes they wore closely resembled the green uniforms of
Napoléon and his two fellow consuls. The comparison was
obvious to all who saw the play. The censor who was responsible for allowing the play to be staged was immediately
dismissed. As for the writer, Dupaty was arrested and ordered to be sent to the Antilles. He was already at Brest when
Josephine and the influential Hugues Maret, who was the
head of the government newspaper *La Moniteur,* finally persuaded Napoléon to release him. Happily Napoléon did not
take such a violent action again. In the future, he would try to
put pressure on the stage in a less high-handed manner. . . .

In 1808, the number of theaters in Paris was further reduced from thirteen to eight. Napoléon established these eight in a sort of hierarchy. The first four, which were directly under the control of the police, were to produce works of major artistic quality; the others were to put on minor works. They also contributed part of their earnings to the upkeep of the major houses. . . .

Even with all these measures, the majority of the French theatrical community actually had a much more harmonious relationship with Napoléon than might at first appear. The majority of playwrights in Napoléonic France were not really desirous of a confrontation with the nation's leader. Most of them saw themselves as craftsmen rather than writers; for many people in France, drama had yet to reach the status of art. Like all craftsmen, the playwrights had to have customers, who for them were their audiences. If they were denied access to this audience, they were denied their means of livelihood. They could not afford to fight great political battles; that had to be left to aristocrats like Chateaubriand and Mme de Staël.

Once the majority of dramatists had grown to accept the fact that Napoléon was going to control the stage, he bore them no grudge. Playwrights who until recently had been critics of the regime did not waste time taking advantage of this benevolence. Dupaty lay low for a few months after his release. But within a year he had returned to the stage. This time, in 1803, instead of satirizing the First Consul, Dupaty presented a play mocking Mme de Staël, a woman who only a year earlier had begged the government for his release from prison. From 1805 on, Dupaty would produce at least two plays a year and would collaborate in the writing of still other dramas. Duval, the author of *Eduard en Ecosse,* which had been such an embarrassment to Napoléon, also was able to produce more plays. In 1811, both Dupaty and Duval, who had once so taunted the regime, now wrote plays that were part of the festivities for the birth of [Napoléon's son] the King of Rome. After the restoration of the Bourbon Monarchy, Dupaty, who had once been nearly shipped off to a penal colony, opened a Bonapartist newspaper.

Theaters nevertheless continued to perform a few plays that were partially critical of Napoléon or poked fun at his policies. Not all dissidents were routed. In 1806, for instance, there was a play that criticized national conscription. But heads of state must always accept a certain amount of public derision; a derision which is not necessarily a political challenge. Besides, with the economic condition of the theaters as it was, such challenges could now be easily controlled. None of the theaters, especially in Paris, were self-sustaining. The most prestigious one, the Opéra, began to receive a government subsidy of as much as 187,716 francs a year in order to maintain it. As a result, the Opéra and other theaters became increasingly dependent upon Napoléon. In this way the state was able to dictate the kind of dramas these institutions would produce.

COURTING PLAYWRIGHTS

Despite all his coercive actions, Napoléon still never lost hope that he might win over the theatrical community willingly. There are two very illuminating examples of this aspiration, the first involving the playwright Jean-François Ducis. Napoléon first met him during the time of the Directory, not long before he departed for Egypt in 1798. Ducis had become very famous for his own version of *Macbeth.* Despite the fact that Napoléon must have seen part of his own life in this play about overweening ambition, he was very impressed and made a concerted effort to win its author over. He even invited the playwright to come with him to Egypt. But like Destutt de Tracy, Ducis was wary of the young general's advances, and rejected the offer. In later years, after Napoléon had taken power, he offered the writer the post of senator and later of poet laureate. Still not wishing to be involved with the regime, Ducis declined these honors. He was not an active opponent of Napoléon, but he made the leader aware that he was a republican and did not wish to be a member of his regime. While thwarted in his efforts to cultivate the strongly principled playwright, the all-powerful Napoléon did not spitefully strike back at him. Instead, Ducis was allowed to continue his writing unmolested.

A second example of Napoléon's effort to court the theatrical community concerns Lemercier, the author of *Pinto.* Despite their political differences, Napoléon had a liking for the playwright. He would often invite Lemercier to Malmaison to dine and also to put on private performances of his plays. The two men would have long talks as they strolled together in the garden, discussing politics and other matters. Despite these amicable relations, however, Lemercier, like Ducis, was a republican and broke with Napoléon after he established the empire in 1804. Napoléon was very disappointed, but once again, he allowed Lemercier to continue to write without any hindrance.

Besides famous playwrights, Napoléon also sought the friendship of the noted tragedians of the day. He was on good terms with Talma, and often sent him letters containing acting tips. When the great performer was portraying Nero in Racine's *Britannicus,* Napoléon advised him, "Your acting should convey more clearly the struggle between an evil disposition and a good education. I also should like you to gesticulate less. Men of Nero's character are not expansive; rather they are concentrated." Later, Napoléon sent Talma some suggestions for his portrayal of Julius Caesar in Corneille's *Mort de Pompée.* "There is a line whose meaning eludes you," he wrote. "You make it sound too sincere: 'To me a throne and infamy are one.' Caesar is not saying he thinks. Do not make Caesar talk like Brutus. When Brutus says that he abhors kings, he should be believed—but Caesar, no. Note the difference."

THEATER AS DIPLOMATIC TOOL

Being very much aware of the influence of drama over public opinion at home, Napoléon was also conscious of the effect it could have abroad. The French theater was therefore often used by Napoléon as a diplomatic device. In 1808, relations between France and Russia were good. Napoléon had reason to believe that he could woo Tsar Alexander I into an alliance, with Paris as the guiding partner. On 9 July 1808, Napoléon wrote to General Louis de Caulaincourt, who at that time was the ambassador to St. Petersburg, to tell him that the tsar was very pleased by the French acting company that was sent to Russia. One of the plays they performed was *Oédipe* by Voltaire. Apparently, Alexander I was very touched by the line "The friendship of a great man is a present from the gods." In 1810, when Napoléon made all the potentates of Europe dance attendance on him at Erfurt, he insisted that they watch the best actors of France perform a selection of his nation's plays. Goethe, who at this time was the director of the Duke of Weimar's theater, was present. When the performances were over, Napoléon invited him into his study to discuss the merits of the various styles of drama. The Emperor spent large sums of money to finance these endeavors. At Erfurt, he procured the services of Talma and Mille by paying them 8,000 and 10,000 francs, respectively, to perform for him. Later, when Napoléon sent the members of the Comédie-Française to perform at Dresden, the capital of Saxony, he paid 111,500 francs to the company as a whole, as well as 10,000 francs to Fleury and 8,000 to Mlle. Georges. Stars did not come cheaply, even for an emperor.

The monarchs who watched Napoléon's actors perform at St. Petersburg, Erfurt, Dresden, and the other capitals of Europe must have believed that he dominated the French stage as he did the continent's politics. But no matter how much Napoléon tried, his goal of establishing a new golden age of French theater remained beyond his grasp. Talent can be nurtured, but it cannot be created. Napoléon's letters and memoranda are replete with examples of his disappointment and anger over his failure to raise the theatrical community to the standards he desired. . . .

It is interesting to note that when Napoléon was incamped at Warsaw during the campaign of 1806–1807 that led up to the Treaty of Tilsit with Russia, he had some of the plays of Kotzebue and other German playwrights translated into French and performed for him privately. These plays may have been banned in France for political reasons, but he was quite aware of their high quality. It must have been with regret that he realized France had nothing to match them. . . .

Napoléon's Conflicting Roles as Censor and Patron

Try as he might, Napoléon could not be both a censor and a patron of the theater at the same time. He often criticized what he judged to be the poor quality of French drama; yet he did not refrain from sometimes using it as an instrument to spread propaganda among the illiterate sections of society. In 1804, for example, he ordered the production of a play on the Battle of Hastings, where England had been conquered by Frenchmen, in order to stir up anti-English feeling among the audience. Napoléon greatly appreciated the dramatic works of the seventeenth century. He once condemned a censor for banning a performance of Molière's *Tartuffe* as someone who "should be a market inspector." Yet it was the Emperor's own policy toward the stage that made this action possible. Napoléon was an admirer of the playwrights of early nineteenth-century Germany. He liked to invite Goethe for dinner and talk about his works. But here, too, art got in the way of his political needs. Goethe's *Faust* was prevented from being produced for the general public because of its suspected nationalist content.

Nevertheless, there are other factors that must be taken into account when making a final evaluation of Napoléon's relationship with the theater. First, at this point in Western history, the dominant creative influence on the stage came from Germany, from such figures as Goethe and Schiller. Even if all censorship and political interference had been removed, France simply did not possess the talent at this time to produce another Racine. Second, Napoléon's attitude to the theater was not that far removed from the attitude that was held in more liberal Britain. Here, Edmund Kean and Mrs. Siddons gained great fame performing bowdlerized versions of Shakespeare. Until 1843, serious drama in Britain was confined to Drury Lane and Covent Garden, while all the nation's other theaters could present only vaudeville and pantomime. It was at least the 1960s before British theaters no longer needed the Lord Chancellor's permission to produce their plays.

Lastly, Napoléon's desire to be both censor and patron led him to follow a policy toward individual playwrights that is innocent when compared to the brutal excesses of authoritarian leaders in this century. With the exception of the Dupaty affair, Napoléon took no violent action against dissidents in the theater. He did a lot of grumbling, he closed down plays he disapproved of; but few writers suffered much personal harm. In fact, many forbidden works were permitted to appear in bookstalls in printed form. Some playwrights were given stern warnings, others were forced to devote part of their talents to writing propaganda, but none had experiences that were in any way similar to those suffered by similar dissidents during the Reign of Terror or in the era of [Adolf] Hitler and [Joseph] Stalin.

Napoléon's censorship cannot be condoned, but it must be put in perspective. His measures did not rob the nation of any great cultural achievements, and when compared to the actions taken in the more progressive countries of the day, were not all that conservative.

Public Opinion: Estrangement and Opposition

Roger Dufraisse

In the following reading from *Napoléon*, author Roger Dufraisse argues that the major reason for Napoléon's downfall was a growing dissatisfaction among the French people. By 1810, when Napoléon had turned forty, his ambitious zeal had slowed considerably, and he preferred spending more time with his wife and baby and less on the details of running the government. Dufraisse explains how Napoléon's withdrawal led to disillusionment throughout the empire among the intellectuals, the upper class, and the clergy. This attitude was at first expressed by a marked increase in trafficking in contraband and desertions from the army, he writes, and later by sporadic but consistent open rebellion. However, Dufraisse maintains that Napoléon, despite enforcing a severe draft and heavy taxation, nevertheless managed to inspire loyalty among the French lower classes—the peasants and artisans—who still felt grateful that he had liberated them from an oppressive feudal system.

In 1810, Napoléon was forty. The most flattering portraits by the court painters did not hide that thickness of feature that made the emperor reflect the decadence of certain of his ancient Roman forbears. But if he was no longer the workaholic who did not know what a full night's sleep was, Napoléon was hardly a broken or exhausted man, as his endurance under the Russian winter and the retreat from Moscow would demonstrate. The superman who used to give all his time to the affairs of state spent the intermission of 1810–1811 with his young wife and infant son. His intellectual powers were fully intact, but less than ever now did he admit to being wrong about anything. Errors were invariably attributed to circumstances or to other people, never to his own miscalculations. Such stubbornness and self-infatuation would prove fatal to him.

GROWING OPPOSITION

Among the causes of Napoléon's downfall must be counted the growing indifference and alienation of public opinion, both within France and without.

"Minor literature is for me; great literature is against me," the emperor used to say, thinking of [influential French political writer and outspoken critic] Madame de Staël and [French Romantic writer René de] Chateaubriand. This was only partly true outside France. Abroad, he sometimes had in his corner writers and publicists of renown. [German writer Johann Wolfgang von] Goethe and [German philosopher Georg] Hegel had been hostile to the Jacobin dictatorship but now hoped for a regeneration of Germany under the leadership of the princes friendly to Napoléon. They followed the imperial regime with interest. In French intellectual circles, the most talented and widely read authors—the liberals, de Staël and Benjamin Constant, and the legitimist (royalist) Chateaubriand—reproached Napoléon for the authoritarian evolution of his regime while maintaining their attachment to public liberties and to property. Though the emperor spared them neither vexations nor annoyances, he had the good sense not to make martyrs of them.

Beyond French borders, intellectual opposition was not only of the salon variety. It fed as much on wounded national pride as on hostility to imperial despotism. In the Confederation of the Rhine, even more especially in the university milieux of Heidelberg and Jena, romantic and nationalist conservatives such as the Schlegel brothers [German scholars August Wilhelm and Friedrich von Schlegel], [Romantic poet] Novalis, and [liberal Catholic writer Joseph von] Goerres denounced Napoléon as the oppressor of the German nation and called on Germans to unite in the fight against him. In Napoléonic Germany, the opposition fed as well on the writings of [influencial political philosopher and journalist Friedrich von] Gentz, who had taken refuge in Vienna, of [German philosopher Johann Gottlieb] Fichte, whose *Speeches to the German Nation* were given in Berlin in 1808, and of [German essayist and poet Ernst Moritz] Arndt. That a liberal such as Madame de Staël would intrigue with so fierce an opponent of the Revolution as the conservative Gentz demonstrates how hatred of Napoléon could unite opposites.

Neither within the empire nor in the allied states did Napoléon succeed in permanently holding on to the loyalty of the upper classes. In France, although the old aristocracy was flattered by his courtship, it stayed secretly legitimist. Outside France, the traditional nobilities (notwithstanding the defection of certain liberal aristocrats in Spain and the Rhine Confederation) never forgave the emperor for taking their privileges away from them. Was not one of Napoléon's most outspoken adversaries [Prussian statesman and reformer] Baron Stein, whose lands had been annexed when the Holy Roman Empire was dismantled?

At first the French clergy had saluted Napoléon as the restorer of the church, but in the vassal states the clergy was more reserved; they persisted in seeing him as the harbinger of the Revolution. Everywhere they deeply resented the loss of the clerical tax (the *dîme),* of their lands, and, in general, the consequences of the policy of secularization to which even legitimate sovereigns had had eager recourse. Nor did the quarrel between the emperor and the pope help matters. In the French empire, a few recalcitrant bishops were imprisoned, and seminarians were subjected to military service. After his imprisonment, Pius VII refused canonical investiture of bishops named by the emperor, thus paralyzing the concordat [1801 treaty between France and the papacy regulating the role of the Roman Catholic Church]. Napoléon replied by reviving Gallicanism [devotion to French culture and tradition]. The Declaration of the Four Articles of 1682 now became the law of the empire. It provided for calling a national council of bishops to consider the question of whether metropolitans had the right, in the absence of paper accord, to invest newly named bishops after a six-month delay. Yet despite their docility in other matters, the French episcopate dug in its heels about breaking with Rome over investiture. Royalists, of course, were delighted with deteriorating church-state relations, but most practicing Catholics were not interested because daily services were not interrupted.

THE BOURGEOISIE

The attitude of the bourgeoisie is harder to ascertain. Certainly in France, Holland, northern Italy, and the Hanseatic cities, shippers and merchants did not forgive Napoléon for ruining maritime commerce. Industrialists were grateful enough to Napoléon for banning British goods, but they protested the scarcity and costliness of sugar and coffee. The average consumer, struck in virtually all his needs for food and clothing by the scarcity of everything from coffee to tobacco to cotton, accumulated a growing list of smoldering grievances against the regime. Finally, the bourgeoisie never forgave Napoléon for removing it from government. Equally out of weariness as out of deliberate calculation, in 1814 the bourgeoisie accepted a liberalized empire that promised the advantages of Bonapartism without the inconveniences.

In the empire and the vassal states, the same forms of popular opposition arose: contraband and desertion. The magnitude of the problem became clearer when, to celebrate Wagram [1809 battle resulting in Napoléon's defeat of Austria], an amnesty was offered to draft dodgers—and 100,000 men applied! On the other hand, placing the phenomenon in perspective, the figures for draft dodging and desertion, though they increased in proportion to the need for men, was no more than 10 percent in 1813. Despite high taxes and conscription, the deeper truth is that the masses were not much affected by the imperial despotism, except during a serious food crisis. The cereal harvest of 1810 was poor, and that of 1811 even worse. The price of bread rose outrageously until the government had to establish a price ceiling [le maximum], a drastic measure not taken since the height of the Jacobin dictatorship in 1793. This crisis coincided with an industrial decline in the autumn of 1810. Beggars and vagabonds spread insecurity in the countryside and caused riots in the cities. A hunger riot in Caen on 2 March 1812 ended with eight death sentences, one of which was passed on a woman. Calm returned only with the good harvest of 1812.

NAPOLÉON MAINTAINS SUPPORT OF LOWER CLASSES

The first armed popular outbursts in the annexed departments did not occur until 1813–1814, and then not everywhere. Often it was the customs officials who were the first victims (as in Hamburg and Amsterdam). Yet on the whole, in France at least (excepting the west and Provence), despite conscription and heavy taxation, the little people, from artisans to peasants, remained staunchly faithful to *l'Empereur* to the end. Did the Hundred Days prove anything less? It was invariably with them that the Napoléonic legend sounded its greatest echo. This was less so in the new departments and in the vassal states, however, especially in those regions where the peasants were not liberated from the feudal regime. (Where they were liberated, as in Germany, for example, they never ceased considering Napoléon their benefactor.)

In certain vassal states, opposition to the Napoléonic grip raised permanent opposition from the majority of the population against the foreign occupier. Beginning in 1809, in Calabria and Apulia [Italy], guerrilla warfare arose, swelled by deserters and draft dodgers and organized by a secret, revolutionary, and xenophobic society: the Carbonaries. The Spanish uprising that began in 1808 permitted England to open an entire second front of warfare as well as to break open the economic blockade.

CHAPTER 3

NAPOLÉON'S FOREIGN POLICIES

PEOPLE
WHO MADE
HISTORY

NAPOLÉON BONAPARTE

The Continental System

Alan Schom

Napoléon's main obstacle to world domination was England, which continually formed military coalitions with other European countries in order to defeat the French emperor. As Alan Schom points out in this selection from his book, *Napoléon Bonaparte*, Britain's refusal to send large armies into battle, coupled with her dominance of the sea, left Napoléon with only one option: destroy the British economy. Toward this end, he arranged an economic blockade of England called the Continental System which prohibited all countries under French control from trading with England. Schom outlines the early success of this plan, as well as its subsequent failure due to Napoléon's alienation of his allies. Schom is also the author of another book about Napoléon, *One Hundred Days*.

Napoléon was determined to break England. If he could not do so on the battlefield, for England never fielded large armies on the Continent, relying instead on a strong navy, then he would follow up the trade war begun during the Revolution.

In 1798 the Directory had ordered the seizure of all neutral vessels that had called on British ports. The British retaliated by taking French colonies and trade through them. Great Britain, as a traditional exporter, depended heavily on colonial products, textiles, and iron products destined for the Continent, while also reliant on corn and timber imports. By 1800 English exports had more than doubled, while imports had risen by 64 percent. In 1803 Napoléon had forbidden trade in British products. After the French navy and merchant marine were irreparably crippled by the decisive

Excerpted from *Napoléon Bonaparte*, by Alan Schom. Copyright © 1997 by Alan M. Schom. Reprinted by permission of HarperPerennial, a division of HarperCollins Publishers, Inc.

naval defeat at Trafalgar in October 1805, Napoléon decided to strike another blow, and in November 1806 issued his Berlin Decree, placing Great Britain under a French blockade. This unique blockade, however, would be enforced by land, not by sea: No ship thereafter was allowed to come directly from British ports or colonies to France or French-controlled ports. England had countered French restrictions by shipping more of its goods under neutral flags, and by 1807, 44 percent of British commerce was thus conveyed. Trade was carefully controlled in London by the selling of export-import licenses. Napoléon tightened the noose on British commerce in November 1807 with his Milan Decree, which required the automatic confiscation of all shipping and goods that had touched English ports. The United States, as a neutral, trading with both France and England, was caught in the middle, attempting to solve the conundrum in 1807 by placing an embargo on trade with both countries.

THE BLOCKADE TAKES A TOLL ON BRITAIN

Despite evasive action by Britain, Napoléon's measures were daily taking a stronger bite. The surest way was through conquest, seizing or controlling one continental power after another and hence those additional ports and markets. He tightened his control of France, the Low Countries, Italy, and central Europe. By 1808 British exports, which two years earlier had reached £40.8 million, dropped to £35.1 million. Violent industrial strikes and shortages of products hurt England, and thus for instance the raw cotton imports reaching Liverpool dropped from 143,000 sacks in 1807 to a mere 23,000 in 1818. Corn imports fell, as did timber, and although British exports to South America rose sharply between 1805 and 1808, from £8 million to £20 million, this often involved onetime sales and irregular payment. On the other hand, British exports to the Mediterranean increased fourfold between 1805 and 1811, particularly in Turkey and Persia. But 1808 had been a very bad year, things only gradually recuperating thereafter. Meanwhile the United Kingdom continued to use neutral shipping when possible, thereby providing sugar, coffee, cotton, and soda for Holland, Frankfurt, and Leipzig. A struggling France tried to compensate for its own loss by introducing grape sugar and linen in place of real sugar and cotton, and by the mandatory planting of one hundred thousand hectares of sugar beets, but Paris failed to close Frankfurt and Leipzig to English products and goods.

Nonetheless 1808 had indeed frightened the British and the French both, as major commercial and banking houses lapsed into bankruptcy. The trade war was double-edged, almost equally destructive to both nations. If Russia was a major partner of Napoléon's Continental System, it also served as an important sieve in Napoléon's system, as Riga and other Baltic ports continued to accept British goods. For all that, France's great commercial war continued greatly to harm the Russian economy.

The year 1811 marked another new low for the British, their exports to the Continent dropping by 80 percent from the previous year, exports to the United States and South America falling by a similar figure. British exports, which had finally risen to £60 million in 1810, had plummeted yet again. Great was the anxiety of the City, and unchecked inflation and poor harvests in 1809 and 1810, aggravated by the flow of English gold to pay its continental allies, only compounded the matter. The coalition against France depended on just such flows of English gold. Bankruptcies swept England again in 1810 and in 1811, resulting in large-scale unemployment or at best reduced three-day workweeks. Many desperate firms and traders blamed not Napoléon but the British government, and on May 11, 1812, a bankrupt businessman by the name of [John] Bellingham walked into the lobby of the House of Commons and shot Prime Minister Spencer Percival. Napoléon rejoiced when he heard the news.

NAPOLÉON ALIENATES HIS ALLIES

Meanwhile a bull-headed Bonaparte, the genius behind this massive economic chaos afflicting Europe, continued to tighten the screws whenever and wherever possible, even when it meant alienating his own allies. In 1810 he officially annexed Holland; the Valais Republic of Switzerland; the Hanseatic cities of Hamburg, Lübeck, Bremen [an organization of north German towns to protect trading interests]; and by January 1811 the Duchy of Oldenburg. That this gravely aggravated Napoléon's relations with the various Germanic states, including those within the Confederation of the Rhine, and Russia in particular, seemed to him quite irrelevant: Napoléon never learned from past mistakes. If his "allies" misbehaved, he could send in [French general Louis-Nicolas, duke of Averstadt] Davout's troops to bully and even occupy them, as indeed he had already done in the case of Hamburg. No one envied that city's fate and the subsequent "war contributions." But that Napoléon chose to do this at a time when events—although stabilizing briefly in 1810—grew more alarming than ever, proved as illogical as it did counterproductive.

England's trade by 1812 was finally improving again, reaching an export figure of £50 million pounds, while France's much-vaunted Continental System could not even begin to equal that. The French economy was sinking desperately, irretrievably. But Napoléon remained intent on destroying the impudent British, regardless of the cost, regardless of the harm to the French and continental economies, and regardless of the destructive cost to his tenuous relations with his political allies and even to his own position.

Ruling the Conquered

Michael Broers

Napoléon fought many great military battles that resulted in entire countries falling under French domination. The real challenge for Napoléon, however,
was not in defeating his enemies on the battlefield,
but in ruling the people who resented their new
leaders. In the following selection, Michael Broers
relates how Napoléon wanted to conquer not only
foreign lands, but also how he wanted to convert
their inhabitants to the French way of life. He describes some of Napoléon's most significant influences, such as the Napoléonic Code, which established a single legal system for all people under
French rule. Although the Napoléonic Code was not
universally welcomed, Broers notes that many of the
conquered came to accept French government. The
author points out that the success or failure of the
French in ruling the conquered depended on having
enough time for the defeated population to recover
from the ravages of war and gain trust in their new
rulers. Broers teaches history at the University of
Leeds in England and is the author of *Europe Under
Napoléon 1799–1815.*

Napoléon was the ruler of a truly European empire and he
devoted enormous energy to governing it, at least as much as
he did to conquering it in the first place. The story of the
'home front'—of what went on behind the frontlines of conflict and conquest—came to embrace the history of all the
peoples of Western and Central Europe in one way or another. The experience of Napoléonic rule—his rise and fall—
proved formative for the collective future of modern Europe.

There are two angles from which the internal history of
the Napoléonic empire must be viewed: from that of the
ruler, and from that of the ruled. The first comprises the

Excerpted from Michael Broers, "The Empire Behind the Lines," *History Today*, vol.
48, no. 1 (January 1998), p. 20–26. Reprinted by permission of *History Today*.

policies Napoléon developed to rule his subjects; the second involves their response to those policies. Only by putting the two together, can any real understanding be gained of the history of the fate of Europe under Napoléon. Even before his grip was secured on any given part of the continent, the experience of war and conquest had, in itself, created circumstances of crucial, often determining, importance for the character of imperial rule that was to follow. The mess created by the military advance of Napoléonic imperialism was the first thing Bonaparte had to deal with, wherever his armies went, just as it was the overwhelming preoccupation of all those he brought under his sway, for in every case, he owed his empire to military conquest, and to that alone.

War was the most widespread, common experience of the peoples of Western and Central Europe at this time. Every area which came into the Napoléonic empire had first to pass through the horrors of war and military occupation. Reduced to its human essentials, this meant that almost all the subject peoples of the empire endured rape and pillage on a grand scale, as a prelude to imperial rule and, when this hard truth is remembered, it is something of a miracle that any semblance of peaceful co-operation ever emerged between the conquered and the invaders. This was even true within France itself, in areas which had seen early counter-revolutionary resistance to the new order, the major example being the Vendée [a royalist and pro-Catholic section of France that unsuccessfully revolted against Napoléon's rule]. But large parts of southern France—the Midi—were also theatres of armed resistance to the Revolution, particularly in the Rhone valley, along the border with Spain, in the Pyrenees and in Provence, the foothills of the Alps.

FEAR AND LOATHING OF THE FRENCH ARMY

When they began their war with the rest of Europe in 1792, the French revolutionary armies had assumed they would be greeted with open arms by the common people of Europe. In fact, the prospect of invasion and occupation stirred much older, atavistic fears among the inhabitants of the Low Countries, the Rhineland, northern Spain, north-western Italy, and the British Isles, all of whom had strong folk memories of earlier wars with France and their attendant atrocities. It was irrelevant what ideological banner the French came under—whether it be that of the aggressive, expansionist Bourbon monarchy of old, or as the 'friends of humanity and the rights of man'—they were still the French, the ancestral, powerful and pitiless enemy.

An Irish traveller in the German Rhineland during the fighting of the 1790s recorded how ordinary people made a direct connection between the fate suffered by their ancestors in the wars against Louis XIV, and their own confrontation with the armies of the French Revolution:

> The particulars of that dismal scene have been transmitted from father to son, and are still spoken of with horror by the peasantry of this country, among whom the French nation is held in detestation to this day.

THE CATHOLIC CHURCH FIGHTS BACK

These latent, almost subconscious fears were fanned, and their forms crystallised, by the propaganda war waged against the Revolution by the Catholic Church, still the greatest single influence on the common people of Western Europe, and their most important source of information about the outside world.

When the French revolutionaries turned the Catholic Church against them—first in 1790, with the Civil Constitution of the Clergy, then with repeated outbursts of religious persecution, which lasted throughout the 1790s—they handed the governments of the surrounding states a powerful propaganda tool, which they employed to considerable effect. When the clergy touched on the deeper, semi-articulated fear of the French harboured by ordinary people, the ground was well presented for ferocious resistance to their advance.

In the end, the Church need not have bothered to stir these embers on behalf of the old order. The violent, rapacious conduct of the French armies was enough to rouse hatred, resentment and resistance on its own. The new 'citizen soldier' of the revolutionary armies saw himself as a citizen of one nation only, France, and when he left its frontiers, he did not carry with him the wider, internationalist aspirations of some revolutionary leaders, such as the Girondins [a political group that supported war as a means to unite the French people behind the cause of the French Revolution]. In his conduct towards non-French peoples, it is clear that the soldier of the Republic had not absorbed the universalism of the original battle-cry of the 'war party' in 1792—'War on the castle, peace to the cottage'—but he had

become imbued with a ferocious sense of French nationalism, which meant a marked sense of superiority towards all
those he encountered.

THE FRENCH SOLDIERS RAVAGE THE LAND

As the war tipped in their favour, French troops found themselves further from home and from their supply bases. Badly
paid and supplied—indeed, often left to 'live off the land' as
a deliberate policy—the revolutionary armies descended on
the rest of Europe like a savage, barbarian horde. The analogy is not an exaggeration, for as time passed, away from
their native villages and families, the troops began to form
loyalties that had less to do with France, itself, and more to
do with their own units. They were 'revolutionised' less by
the efforts of government propaganda, than by this sense of
rootlessness, reinforced by a reciprocal hatred for foreign
populations which resisted them, often by cruel means, and
by other aspects of government policy.

Just as the French soldier often did not divorce the political cause he defended from the quest for booty and supplies,
so the civilian populations he invaded did not distinguish
between the behaviour of the French troops and the revolution they carried with them. This hate-filled interaction began in earnest in the Vendée, and during the suppression of
the Federalist revolts of 1793-94 when the large southern
cities rose against Paris. It was nurtured within France itself,
but as the armies pushed forward, it became a phenomenon
of European dimensions.

In the context of the Napoléonic empire, perhaps the
most important point to bear in mind—and it is often forgotten—is that this process was, truly, 'ongoing'. It did not
end with the change of regime in 1799, nor did it soften in
any way, as time progressed. Napoléon made many com-
promises with the enemies of the Revolution, as shall be
seen, but he never allowed this to touch the armies. He
made sure they remained bastions of republicanism; in so
far as they had clear political views, the troops were just as
imbued with anti-clericalism and hatred of the old order, as
in the 1790s. Perhaps the clearest evidence of this is that
Napoléon never allowed his troops to have chaplains with
them, in accordance with revolutionary tradition. The
armies became more, not less, cut off from the peasant society they had left behind, after 1799, and they remained

just as contemptuous of the new populations they encountered, with every military success.

'INNER' VS. 'OUTER' EMPIRE

What changed after 1799 was not the conduct and attitude of the armies or the peoples who had to endure their presence, but rather that the battlelines moved away from the original fronts, around the eastern and southern borders of France. The war and its attendant horrors shifted from the Low Countries, western and central Germany and northern and central Italy, and with this the French—at last—saw the chance to create a new stability, on their own terms, a chance to clean up their own mess. The 'war syndrome' moved on: to Spain and Portugal in 1808—where the French, themselves, continued to compare circumstances to the Vendée—and to the North Sea and Adriatic coasts and southern Italy, where a 'monstrous little war' raged until 1814 between the French and the bandits of Calabria. These last named regions became the outer fringe of the 'Grand Empire', never really absorbed by Napoléon, and always the scenes of bitter guerrilla wars.

By contrast, those areas first conquered and furthest from the fighting, became an 'inner' empire, where French rule was stable and secure for most of the period 1801–12. It is essential to grasp this distinction within Napoléon's territories, for it is far more important than the largely artificial differences between satellite kingdoms, allied states and the non-French departments, ruled directly from Paris. Whereas the latter were the makeshift creations of improvised diplomacy, the concept of 'inner' and 'outer' empires rests on genuine, practical levels of stability and control.

In the lands of the 'inner empire', it became possible to create a stable, civilian administrative system of local government, based on the prefects, and to allow the laws of the Napoléonic Civil Code to operate in full, with all the guarantees for the protection of persons and property they allowed. These areas settled into relative peace and security early in the period, and this was where the Napoléonic reforms in justice and administration really took root. This happened directly in those vast parts of Western Europe annexed to France, including much of western Germany and north-western Italy, as well as all of modern Belgium—and by imitation in the satellite kingdoms of Italy—centred on Milan, and in Holland, or in those states closely allied with France, such as Bavaria, Baden and Wurtemberg in southern Germany.

THE NAPOLÉONIC CODE IN CONQUERED COUNTRIES

The broad outlines of the centralised administrative system devised in France during the Revolution, and the general concepts of the Napoléonic Code had become 'the norms' in these parts of Europe by the fall of Napoléon in 1814. The Code brought an end to the power of the guilds to regulate many aspects of working life, and almost complete freedom of profession; it brought equality before the law for all citizens, where it was applied in full—which it was not in Bavaria, where Jews were still denied full civil rights—and the equal division of property among all citizens. Many of these changes were far from welcomed by ordinary people, as they represented the destruction of numerous deeply-rooted customs and traditions, and often spelled the loss of important privileges, not just for the nobility, but for whole cities and provinces. No one was exempt from the ferocious conscription laws Napoléon imposed on his own state and all his allies, to raise his massive armies. However, the long period of stability between 1801 and 1812 made millions of Western Europeans accustomed to both the good and the bad aspects of Napoléonic methods of government.

Napoléon sought to apply the same sets of policies to all the territories he came to control, regardless of when he seized them or whether he ruled them directly, as French departments, by proxy in his satellite kingdoms, or by indirect pressure, as in the independent, allied states of the Confederation of the Rhine. How successful he was depended essentially on how well a given part of his empire got over the initial shock of its conquest by his armies. Put another way, it depended on how much time his officials had to repair the ravages of war and win the trust of those they administered. Broadly, they made some progress in the lands of the 'inner empire', but they failed beyond them, in the areas Napoléon seized after about 1806.

In Spain, central and southern Italy, the northern coast of Germany, the Adriatic coast of modern Croatia, and in the 'Grand Duchy of Warsaw'—the core of modern Poland—Napoléonic rule was disruptive and traumatic. Usually, it brought with it only the horrors of war, conscription and heavy taxation, with none of the benefits felt further west. To this day, in Slovenia, peasants call taxes *fronki*—'French'—a sign of how Napoléonic rule is remembered in the more far flung parts of the 'Grand Empire'. In total contrast, when Prussia acquired most of the Rhineland at the Congress of Vienna in 1814, its rulers wisely decided to allow the region to retain almost all of the Napoléonic Code, because for the propertied and educated classes, at least, it had come to be regarded as a guarantee of civil liberties.

Attitudes to policing followed a similar pattern to the reception of the laws it enforced. Within the lands of the 'inner empire', the Gendarmerie—a paramilitary police force devoted to policing the countryside—proved popular and durable, at least among the better-off and isolated peasant communities. The Gendarmes were hated as the enforcers of conscription, but they also assured basic order where once banditry had been rife. Consequently, they were imitated or retained in many countries after the end of Napoléonic rule. The Netherlands and many Italian states retained Gendarmeries after 1814, while the Prussians adopted many of their methods.

SPAIN RESISTS FRENCH RULE

The contrast with Spain, however, is striking. Here, French rule provoked the massive people's war against Napoléon, called the *guerrilla*. This true 'war of liberation' may have been a glorious chapter in Spanish history, but it had the devastating side-effect of turning a once peaceful country into a sea of banditry, as the guerrilla bands, the *partidas*, often refused to return to normal life and turned to crime, with no effective police force to cope with them. All over Europe, millions of soldiers were 'demobilised' in the years after 1814, usually returning to civilian life at a time of economic recession and poor harvests; yet in most of the lands of the 'inner empire', a semblence of civil order was maintained in the face of these difficult circumstances. In Spain, however, the collapse of all effective administration led to disorder on a huge scale that was not mastered for decades to come.

None of this meant that Napoléonic officials did not try to enforce the imperial system of government in these 'frontier' regions. In the Spanish Pyrenees, one young French prefect, Viefville, sent to govern an area infested with rebels was not even able to enter the main town of his department for the first eight months of his appointment in 1812. Once there, he had a serious nervous breakdown. Yet Viefville recovered, stayed at his post to the end, and did what he could to better the area, building a hospital and introducing proper sanitation methods to the town. Ultimately, however, he failed to make any real impact on the region; the war was always too close and the local rebels too strong for him.

TENSIONS IN THE INNER EMPIRE

Clearly, it depended very much on where you were, as to whether you saw any of the benefits of Napoléonic rule. Even within the 'inner empire' there were always tensions between its positive and negative aspects which made the impact of the Napoléonic state very much a mixed blessing, even in its heartlands. Conscription cast a shadow over most parts of Europe Napoléon controlled. Indeed, the French regarded their ability to raise men from a particular area as the benchmark of whether they really had a grip on it or not. Outside France itself, northern Italy, Belgium and the German states, became reliable sources of recruits, whereas the French never dared introduce it in the Kingdom of Naples—the southern half of the Italian peninsula—or in those parts of Spain they controlled. Even within France, itself, Napoléon exempted the volatile western region centred on the Vendée for as long as he could and, after 1812, kept its quotas low; along the border with Spain, it broke down altogether by the end of his rule.

Everywhere, conscription was hated, even in the heart of France itself. The novelist, Alfred de Musset was a schoolboy during the Napoléonic wars, and has left us this vivid impression in his memoirs:

> During the wars of the Empire . . . worried mothers brought a . . . nervous generation into the world, conceived between two battles, brought up in colleges to the role of drums, thousands of children looked around at each other with sombre eyes . . . Every year France made a present to this man (Napoléon) of 300,000 youths . . . Never were there so many sleepless nights as in the time of this man; never were there to be seen, leaning over the ramparts of town walls, such a nation of sorrowing mothers; never did such silence envelop those who spoke of death.

Napoléon had many battles to fight on his 'home front' and, on one level, he won several of them, at least within the 'inner empire'. Life was regulated by a clear, rational and usually fair legal code. In what has become the core of the modern European Union, all these characteristics of the Napoléonic empire can still be seen at work, because they did just that—work. However, it took the end of the wars, and the suffering they brought, even well behind the lines, for these benefits to become obvious to most of the ordinary people of Europe. Nevertheless, by the 1820s and 1830s, it was clear to most educated Europeans that the best way to run a state efficiently was still very close to the models Napoléon had introduced them to.

A New France in America

Paul Fregosi

Four years after Napoléon came to power, France finally managed to regain the Louisiana Territory that Louis XV had given to Spain thirty years earlier. As Paul Fregosi explains in this excerpt from his book, *Dreams of Empire: Napoléon and the First World War 1792–1815*, Napoléon hoped to build another New France to replace the Canadian territory that had been lost to Britain forty years earlier—and then to dominate the North American continent. When British ships became a looming threat to France, Fregosi details the emperor's realization that he would need to abandon his dream of a New France and concentrate on defeating England.

Before the loss of Canada to the British [in 1763] and of Louisiana to the Spanish [in 1762], France had ruled, if only nominally, over most of the vast and empty spaces of North America west of the Appalachians, all the way to the Rockies, up to the Great Lakes and the endless prairies, down to the Gulf of Mexico. Louisiana then was many, many times larger than the state which bears that name today. . . .

The French government had decided the time was ripe for the territory to return to France and thus restore France to her former eminence in the New World. Spain, partly occupied by French troops, haggled, hummed and hawed over the matter. It was not until Napoléon Bonaparte became First Consul and the no-nonsense ruler of France four years later that Spain finally agreed to let the territory go.

Weak and divided as Spain then was, she really had no option. But in exchange the French handed over to the Spanish royal family the Italian Duchy of Parma and Etruria, and there were many well-placed people in the Spanish court who were delighted at the deal.

Negotiations over the transfer of Louisiana continued between the two countries from July 1800 until its cession was confirmed by the Treaty of San Ildefonso, on October 1, 1801. When the people of New Orleans heard that Louisiana was becoming French again, they sang the 'Marseillaise' in the streets and coffee houses. For them it was a homecoming after nearly forty years of Spanish rule.

Napoléon had made peace with Great Britain in October 1801 and, a year earlier, with the United States with whom France had been in a state of half-war. The way to Louisiana therefore was now clear. The ocean between Europe and North America was wide open to commerce and travel again. The British navy was no longer in the way.

SPAIN IS HAPPY TO BE RID OF LOUISIANA

Strangely enough the Spaniards, and specially the court and government, were not displeased at returning the territory to the French. Louisiana was a huge wilderness of snakes, swamps, prairies and wild Indians, with perhaps fifty thousand white settlers in all, and it was far from Spain. Tuscany, in delightful, highly civilised Italy and only a few days' travel from Madrid, had a population of over one million, and would bring its ruler a more than adequate revenue. 'Frankly, Louisiana costs us more than it is worth,' the Spanish foreign minister Mariano Urquijo wrote to his ambassador in Paris. Louisiana's deficit was trimming nearly $340,000 from the Spanish Treasury every year.

The Spaniards, moreover, were already worried over United States expansionism. Americans were beginning to swarm into the Mississippi region. In a period of just two months, in September and October 1795, Kentucky and Tennessee each received nearly thirty thousand new settlers, and these regions were only separated from Louisiana territory by a river's width. The Spaniards knew their big problem would be to keep the Americans out.

By 1800 the position had become even more troubling. 'It would be very useful to place a barrier between the Americans and ourselves, a barrier against their plans of colonisation, by means of a nation like France,' the Spanish foreign minister pointed out in his letter to his Paris ambassador, detailing the positive aspects for Spain of the cession of Louisiana to France.

PLANS FOR A NEW FRANCE

Napoléon's new dream was taking shape. The dream was to build a new New France, to replace the old New France of Canada, lost to the British forty years before. This new New France would link the islands of the Caribbean, Martinique, St Lucia, Guadeloupe, Tobago, Haiti and the whole of the island of Hispaniola to the Mississippi valley, with New Orleans the vital point in the middle, and then on up north to Canada, skirting the Rockies to the west and the Mississippi River to the east, all the way to the Great Lakes and east down the St Lawrence River to Quebec and Acadia. It was a grand dream. It was not only a New France that would come into being. It was a New World, a French-speaking world. The other occupants of the North American continent, Britain, the United States and Spain, would be completely overshadowed. Napoléon's ambitions were never mean. . . .

On June 2, 1802, he wrote to Admiral [Denis] Decrès, his navy minister, that he intended 'to take possession of Louisiana with the shortest possible delay.' A list of civil officers for Louisiana was drawn up, headed by a colonial prefect, Pierre Clément de Laussat. Some five thousand troops prepared for embarkation at Dunkirk. In August, General [Marshal] Victor . . . was appointed captain-general of Louisiana, and given the command of the expeditionary corps and a salary of seventy thousand francs a year.

FRANCE SEEKS ALLIANCE WITH NATIVE AMERICANS

Napoléon Bonaparte forgot neither the native Indians nor the threat from the nearby Americans, particularly those whom he described as the 'Western Americans', the pioneers and frontiersmen who were already moving into the virtually untouched lands bordering the Mississippi River to the east, and who caused the Spaniards so much worry. 'We must also strengthen ourselves against the Western Americans by forming alliances with the Indian nations scattered on the east side of the river. The Chickasaws, Choctaws, Alabamans, Creeks, etc, are said to be entirely devoted to us,' the First Consul wrote in his instructions to Victor.

To cultivate Indian friendship was important, and a large quantity of presents for the Redskins were packed for shipment. They included two hundred special medals as gifts for friendly Indian chiefs and witch doctors. On one

side the medal bore the effigy of First Consul Bonaparte.
On the other, the words: 'To Loyalty'. Whose loyalty to
whom is not clear.

Of more practical interest to the Indians would be the
5,000 muskets, 150 rifles, 20,000 pounds of powder, 1,000
swords and 5,000 tomahawks. There was enough there to
do plenty of damage. Had Napoléon secured Louisiana,
quite a few American scalps would have garnished the local
Indian huts.

POLITICAL PROBLEMS CAUSE FRANCE TO RECONSIDER

In October 1802 it was decided that the expeditionary force for
Louisiana should leave from the Dutch port of Helvoet Sluys,
near Rotterdam, instead of Dunkirk as originally planned. . . .

At Christmas the fleet was still not ready to sail. Victor
was concerned as the winter threatened to be exceptionally cold, but he required two or three more weeks in
which to bring up essential supplies from Dunkirk. Then
the fleet could depart. But the fleet never sailed. Early in
January the harbour waters froze and remained frozen
until the end of February. The French ships could not stir
from their anchorage. Relations between France and
Britain were worsening. The First Consul had a dreadful
row with Lord Whitworth, the British ambassador, at a
public reception in Paris. The British fleet began pa-
trolling off the Dutch coast.

These may have been months of inactivity in Helvoet
Sluys for the French expedition but elsewhere, in Washington, Paris, London, Madrid, New Orleans and on the ocean,
events were moving and messengers were rushing to and
fro, as fast as the galloping hooves of horses and North At-
lantic winds could make them.

In Spain, after finagling for better conditions, King
Charles IV, with the connivance of his prime minister,
Manuel Godoy, who slept with the Queen and styled himself
The Prince of Peace, had at last signed on October 15, 1802,
the Royal Order making over Louisiana to the French.

In London, in the usual lofty British diplomatic ambiguous tone, Lord Hawkesbury dismissed French accusations
that the British ships were blockading the French expedition. The British naval vessels, he said, had been ordered not
to make 'any movements or hold any language which could
be regarded as being of a hostile nature.'

U.S. ATTITUDE TOWARD FRANCE

In the United States, President Jefferson viewed the reoccupation of Louisiana by France with great misgivings. 'The possessor of Louisiana is our natural enemy,' he wrote to Robert Livingston, the United States ambassador in Paris. The return of the French on the North American continent 'works most sorely with the United States,' he added. Never mind that it was largely with French money that the United States of America had won its independence twenty years earlier. National self-interest has no time for gratitude, as the Americans have since discovered for themselves. That's the way of the world.

'The day that France takes possession of New Orleans . . . we must marry ourselves to the British fleet and nation,' Jefferson told Livingston, in an obvious reference to a possible British-US alliance directed against France. Yet Jefferson was pro-French, or at least as pro-French as it is possible for an American to be, and a liberal who backed many of the principles of the French Revolution. But he didn't want France as a neighbour. France was too strong. Perhaps he too was already feeling the itch of 'manifest destiny' and wanted North America, all of it, for his fellow-Americans.

In the meantime, he authorised Livingston to offer $10 million to France for New Orleans and a strip of territory beside the Mississippi, and sent his friend and former law student James Monroe to Paris to assist the US envoy in his negotiations. Monroe already knew France well. He had been US minister in Paris from 1794 to 1796.

New Orleans, at the mouth of the Mississippi, had become a vital outlet for the United States of America. The port was used largely for shipping lumber, furs, cotton, tobacco and grain and, to the indignation of all, this navigational right (guaranteed by the 1783 Treaty of Paris) was temporarily suspended in 1802 by the Spanish authorities who were continuing, with France's accord, to govern the territory in the name of the still absent captain-general, General Victor.

His temporary replacement, De Laussat, arrived in New Orleans on March 26,1803. He had come on ahead on the French ship, *Le Surveillant,* from the ice-free port of La Rochelle to represent France while Victor and his five-thousand-man army remained stuck in the Dutch ice.

Somewhere at sea, without sighting each other, the westward-bound *Le Surveillant* and an eastward-bound

American brig passed each other in mid-ocean hundreds of miles apart. The United States vessel was taking to France President Jefferson's special envoy, James Monroe, to arrange the purchase of New Orleans from the French while the French ship was bringing Pierre-Clément de Laussat to New Orleans to take the city and territory over for France! . . .

NAPOLÉON DECIDES TO SELL LOUISIANA

It must have been some time in March 1803, with war at hand and British ships off the Dutch coast, that Napoléon Bonaparte finally realised he had no chance of sending his army to Louisiana. Relations with Britain were becoming more and more tense. The Treaty of Amiens required the British to evacuate Malta, but they were refusing, and at the same time accusing France of maintaining troops in Switzerland, as well as in Italy and the Netherlands. The two countries were headed, once again, for war.

The First Consul concluded that since he would be unable to defend Louisiana against the British his only practical solution might be to sell the territory to the Americans. But first, on the evening of April 10, he summoned for consultation two of his ministers: Minister of the Treasury, François Barbé-Marbois, and Minister for the Navy and the Colonies, Admiral Decrès.

Decrès, fat, cynical and supercilious, usually strongly opposed to distant military campaigns, this time spoke passionately in favour of fighting for Louisiana. He urged Bonaparte to keep Louisiana French. It was Barbé-Marbois who was in favour of selling. He thought the money would be useful. He had lived in America and his wife was American. The three men talked far into the night.

The next day, Bonaparte announced his decision: he would sell. But he would sell not only New Orleans, which the Americans were demanding anyway, but the whole of Louisiana, all the way from the Gulf of Mexico to the Great Lakes and to the Rockies. France was departing from North America, abandoning Louisiana as it had abandoned Canada.

'The British have twenty ships of war in the Gulf of Mexico. I have not a moment to lose to put Louisiana out of their reach,' Napoléon Bonaparte impatiently told the French diplomats who were negotiating with the Americans.

The British navy by its very existence and without even firing a shot won perhaps its most important victory of all time on the day of the famed Louisiana Purchase. But the victory was for the United States, not for England.

After Bonaparte's decision to sell the territory there remained one obstacle to the deal: Livingston, the American envoy to France. The American minister in Paris was empowered only to negotiate the purchase of New Orleans, not the whole of Louisiana. Barbé-Marbois, on the other hand, insisted that the sale was a package deal, New Orleans plus the rest of Louisiana, a territory as large as the then United States. It would double the size of the country. All for eighty million francs, just over eleven million dollars. It came to four cents an acre.

Startled and confused, Livingston asked for time to think. The next day Jefferson's friend James Monroe arrived in Paris. The timing was unplanned but for the Americans it was superb.

There was nothing small-minded about Monroe. He at once visualised the continental dimensions his country would acquire, literally between one day and the next. He gave his agreement immediately. The next three weeks were spent discussing the details.

The deed of sale—how better can we term the Louisiana Purchase Treaty?—was signed in Paris on April 30, 1803. On that day the United States acquired a territory nearly four times the size of France, covering in whole or in part thirteen of today's states: Louisiana, Arkansas, Missouri, Oklahoma, Kansas, Iowa, Nebraska, Minnesota, South and North Dakota, Montana, Wyoming and Colorado. Three weeks later Britain and France were at war.

Nothing Napoléon Bonaparte ever did had more far-reaching effects than selling Louisiana to the Americans. By thus propelling the United States into the front rank of nations considerably sooner than would otherwise have been the case—maybe by a century or more—he transformed world history. . . .

As he had said he would, Napoléon Bonaparte used most of the proceeds from the sale of Louisiana to finance his proposed invasion of the British Isles. He armed, trained, equipped, fed and paid tens of thousands of men who didn't fight for two years but camped instead on the Channel shores, staring out across a few dozen miles of water to where the untested English enemy was preparing to repulse them. With the money, Napoléon also built thousands of invasion craft which never went to sea. Most of the boats rotted away with age. French Louisiana lies in the ooze and the mud at the bottom of Boulogne harbour. . . .

On November 30, the Spaniards ceremonially handed Louisiana over to the French. Three weeks later, on December 20, in a similar military ritual De Laussat passed it on to the two American representatives, the soft-spoken Governor [William C.C.] Claiborne, governor of the territory of Mississippi who came down from Natchez for the ceremony, and General James Wilkinson, who was later involved in Aaron Burr's traitorous attempt to break the south-west away from the United States. The French flag was slowly hauled down and the Stars and Stripes raised on the flagstaff. The Louisiana Militia presented arms and one of its officers, accompanied by sixty of his comrades, carried the folded French flag to the downcast De Laussat and Colonel [André] Burthe for safekeeping. 'We shall always remain attached to France,' he said. Many of the Louisianians were in tears. They were no longer French but American citizens and, to be frank, they didn't like it.

A similar ceremony was held on March 9, 1804, at St Louis, on the Missouri river, in Upper Louisiana. From St Louis that year, at the order of President Jefferson, the Lewis and Clark expedition set out to seek a route to the Pacific Ocean. The United States had become a continental power and, for France, the American Dream was over.

CHAPTER 4

NAPOLÉON'S MILITARY CAREER

Changing Modern Warfare

Robert B. Holtman

Napoléon is one of the most studied and admired military strategists in history. Every major war since his rule has featured strategies he employed on the battlefield. In the following reading from *The Napoléonic Revolution*, Louisiana State University history professor Robert B. Holtman contends that much of Napoléon's military success was a direct result of innovations and theories that were already in progress, in part due to the French Revolution. Napoléon's genius, Holtman explains, was in incorporating all those principles and applying them on a much larger scale than the theorists themselves had envisioned. Holtman shows how Napoléon, beyond being a great general, capitalized on his victories through extensive propaganda that exaggerated his triumphs and downplayed his defeats. Holtman is also the author of *Napoléonic Propaganda*.

The name "Napoléon" almost automatically evokes a mental picture of a short man with right hand tucked inside his coat or jacket. Next arises the concept of Napoléon as a military leader—perhaps as a ruthless conqueror, perhaps as romantically pictured by court painter Jacques-Louis David, on horseback crossing the Alps in winter. (Actually Napoléon sat on a mule led by a soldier.)

That first thoughts turn to the military side of Napoléon's career is not surprising. More glamor generally attaches to the military man than to the civilian, and Napoléon was at war for all but fourteen months of the almost fifteen years he was in power.

NAPOLÉON'S INFLUENCE ON MILITARY TACTICS

As early as 1817 the United States Army cadets at West Point began to study Napoléon in a course on "The History of the Art of War." Today Napoléon is still studied at West Point, where a knowledge of his work is considered as important in this age of nuclear weapons as it was earlier. . . .

Why this continued emulation of Napoléon? Not because he was a great military innovator, for he tended to be conservative. But he was the first to incorporate and apply all the principles devised by the military writers of the 18th century; later he extended them to larger operations than they had in mind. . . .

Points agreed on by most of the writers were incorporated into the Ordinance of 1791 for infantry. This ordinance was the basis of infantry tactics (*tactics* being that branch of military science and art which deals with disposing and maneuvering forces after close contact has been established with the enemy) during the wars of the French Revolution and the Napoléonic period. It provided for a "mixed order," calling for marching in column up to the attack, since columns were much more maneuverable than lines, and then swinging into a flexible alternation of columns and three-rank lines. Thus it represented a compromise between the champions of the two sides. The ordinance allowed leeway, recognizing that the terrain might demand tactics different from those normally prescribed. It also placed reliance on the *élan* of the French troops; but this was not a radical innovation, as writer after writer in the 18th century had found more spirit in the French troops than in their enemies.

The conception of the cavalry's role also changed in the latter part of the 18th century. The cavalry came to be considered purely a shock weapon rather than another armed force. In order to fulfill its new role, it had to depend on speed; to attain the desired swiftness required relatively more attention to quality and less to quantity.

It was also in the 18th century that artillery received an independent status. By the end of the century military men realized that artillery should be concentrated against a decisive point in the enemy's position, either that from which he might attack, or the one where he was most vulnerable to attack. The French had made their artillery more mobile than that of any other country.

When Napoléon put into practice this fund of experience

Napoléon, one of the most studied and admired military strategists in history, is depicted planning another campaign.

and expert theory, the mixed order, calling for a combination of shock- and fire-power, remained his favorite tactical organization. Although he grumbled for years about the uselessness of the third rank, he waited until the battle of Leipzig in 1813 before eliminating it and using a two-line front to obtain maximum firepower. At least in the early years he relied heavily on skirmishers to keep the enemy off-balance so his own troops could arrange their battle formations; later, when the recruits were no longer so well trained, he relied on preparatory artillery fire. Basically, however, he was interested in strategy—the science and art of using time and space to meet the enemy under advantageous conditions—and he excelled in getting his men to the decisive place at the right time. He drove home the necessity of advance planning to achieve desired results:

> A consecutive series of great actions is never the result of chance and luck; it is always the product of planning and genius.

> A plan of campaign should take into consideration everything the enemy can do and prescribe the necessary measures to counteract him. Plans of campaign may be modified ad infinitum according to circumstances, the genius of the commander, the character of the troops, and the topography of the theater of war.

TROOP SPEED CHANGES WARFARE

To Napoléon the entire aim of the tactical changes had been to gain greater mobility and maneuverability: "The strength of an army, like power in mechanics, is the product of the mass by the velocity. A rapid march augments the morale of an army, and increases its means of victory." He was inspired with the idea of mobility, which enabled him repeatedly to surprise his enemies. "War is composed of nothing but surprises. While a general should adhere to general principles, he should never lose the opportunity to profit by these surprises." This point he stressed in all his early and successful campaigns. When he marched against the Austrian general Karl Mack at Ulm in the fall of 1805, he reached his goal in less than half the time Mack thought it would take the French to move from the English Channel.

Napoléon's campaigns were the early versions of the 20th-century blitzkrieg, or lightning warfare. He tried to operate on interior lines so as to be able, by having less distance to move, to strike anywhere along the line, and even to maneuver into the enemy's rear and sever his line of communications. Napoléon was a master of diversions to feint the enemy out of position. One reason for his practice of living off the country was to avoid being bound to magazines (depots of military supplies) as 17th- and 18th-century generals had been; traveling light, his army could travel fast. This practice had its weaknesses: it was most suitable to a fertile area, and it demanded a short campaign. But only with him was a system of mobile warfare fully realized.

The speed with which Napoléon moved permitted him to gain the advantage in several ways. He was interested in enveloping the enemy, much as the pincers attacks of World War II attempted this same maneuver. Speed of movement also permitted him on many occasions to turn the enemy's flank; doing so was one of his aims, for the flank is always more vulnerable than the front, and an attack on it tends to cause confusion among troops on the defensive. Napoléon also chose, whenever possible, a point of attack which would divide the enemy forces, who were often from different states; the fact that he was fighting against a coalition frequently made his task easier. He could also concentrate his own forces before the enemy was able to take the same step and before making contact with his opponent. "A union of various bodies must never be made near the enemy, because the enemy by concentrating his forces may not only prevent their junction but may beat them separately." Because of his ability to move and strike swiftly, Napoléon dared to disperse his troops in the knowledge that he could reunite them when necessary. Conversely, dispersion of the divisions permitted greater mobility.

Napoléon's dispersion of his troops came from the realization, which he was the first to hold, that divisions were large enough to be self-sufficient. During the French Revolution and Napoléonic period, armies became larger. Divisions—and after 1800, corps—replaced regiments as the major unit. After 1805 even the corps had a full complement only of infantry; engineers joined the cavalry and heavy guns in a central reserve. As a concomitant of self-sufficiency, Napoléon granted corps commanders a greater degree of freedom than under earlier commanders or under [Arthur Wellesley, Duke of] Wellington [British commander who later defeated Napoléon at Waterloo]. This self-sufficiency meant that divisions could be dispersed and still be supporting one another. Brigades could be shifted from division to division as needed. The rules of support which others, such as the writers, had glimpsed only for divisional purposes Napoléon extended to an entire theater—just as he did the rules for the rise of terrain.

These are the main values for the military student today—to see how highly mobile units of moderate size but powerfully armed were able to operate independently. Napoléon was the first to grasp the principles of organized dispersion and apply them in a way permitting concentration when that was desirable.

Interested in mobility, Napoléon did not concern himself overmuch about his line of communications with France. But the line of operations, extending from the front to the city serving temporarily for the direction of rear operations, did vitally concern him: "An army must have but one line of operations. This must be maintained with care and abandoned only for major reasons."

NAPOLÉON'S MOST INFLUENTIAL CAMPAIGNS

Which of Napoléon's battles and campaigns are most studied for positive rather than negative reasons? First comes the Italian campaign of 1796–97, in which he cleverly separated the Sardinian and Austrian forces and attacked them in the rear. The Austerlitz campaign revealed in masterly fashion how to utilize and move inferior numbers so as to have superiority at the decisive points. The pursuit of the Prussians after Jena is classic; in three weeks the French captured 140,000 prisoners and virtually wiped out the Prussian army. Friedland revealed Napoléon's ability to seize the advantage on ground with which he was not familiar. And in the 1814 campaign in France he exploited in masterly fashion the interior lines of communication.

Napoléon was in several respects a forerunner of the 20th-century world wars. He used the artillery to prepare the way for infantry attacks. He demanded fire superiority, as the writers had stressed, in order not to be disorganized or destroyed by the enemy's fire before reaching the enemy. Unlike his predecessors, he did not preach the conservation of ammunition, especially not for the artillery. He complained that the artillery did not fire enough—that it should fire continuously without calculating expenditure. He tried to give the guns enough rounds, approximately three hundred, for two battles, and the field commanders were expected to use these to the best possible advantage. At Toulon in 1793 Bonaparte employed massed artillery for siege purposes with great effectiveness. Yet it was not until 1808 that he used mass artillery on the battlefield. In part the delay resulted from the fact that in the early campaigns his armies were so superior in quality and his tactics and strategy so surpassed his enemies' that he did not need to place such reliance on artillery.

He anticipated the World War II idea of a theater commander. "Nothing is more important in war than unity of command. Thus, when war is waged against a single power, there must be but one army, acting on one line and led by one chief." As early as May 1796 be wrote the Directory from Italy after receiving a letter urging that he turn south and leave an army under [Gen. François-Christophe] Kellermann [commander of the Army of the Alps] around Milan:

> If you weaken your power by dividing your forces, . . . you will lose the finest opportunity to impose your rule in Italy. Everyone has his own method of waging war. General Kellermann has more experience and would do better than I, but the two of us together would do very badly.

In Paris, Bonaparte told the Directory early in 1798 that "The whole of the navy situated in the area of the Army of England must, like the other arms, be entirely in the hands of the general commanding the Army.". . .

CONSCRIPTION BUILDS FRENCH ARMY

The French Revolution saw a *levée en masse*, a conscription of all resources and making all elements of the population liable for service. In the Year VI (1798) the Directory passed a draft law for men aged twenty to twenty-five; it exempted married men, divorced men who were heads of families, and widowers. Conscription did not work very well during the Revolution; only one third of the conscripts ever reported. Bonaparte put teeth into the draft laws and made them work. From 1799 through 1805 2,000,000 were classed for conscription, and 1,250,000 called up. One fourth of all those called were rejected on physical grounds; Napoléon exempted those who supported families, and after the promulgation of the Concordat with the Papacy in 1802 exempted seminarians. The number actually serving reached 700,000. In 1805 he replaced the local draft boards with prefects and subprefects, and by 1807 almost 100 per cent of the desired number of recruits reached the army. One reason is that Napoléon permitted draftees to obtain substitutes; as the campaigns became more dangerous, the price rose, until in 1812 it was 15,000 francs, ten times as high as in 1805. In 1812 and 1813 half the eligible men escaped serving in the army.

Although his demands, particularly after 1812, were heavy, Napoléon recruited within the 1789 borders of France only 2.1 million men in all the years he was in power. This figure did not represent a debilitating effect on the post-Napoléonic French male population; the population of France showed a considerable rise, in part because the draft led to early marriages. Ironically, his last army, in 1815, broke with the Revolutionary tradition Napoléon had inherited and followed. He was afraid to resort to conscription, or even to amalgamate the national guard and the regular army.

Napoléon differed from earlier generals in his success at raising, organizing, and equipping mass armies. These armies were made possible first of all by the improved roads of the 18th century; the better roads had been used initially, however, merely to transport more baggage per soldier rather than larger armies and heavier equipment such as guns. Secondly, even though Napoléon's factories were not capable of producing enough guns to build up a satisfactory reserve supply, the industrial revolution made it possible to turn out the vast numbers of items needed by a mass army. With it we have the start of modern war.

NAPOLÉON'S INNOVATIONS

For what kind of innovations should Napoléon be given credit? First, for making propaganda a regular arm of the military. He clearly recognized the importance of morale. We shall see later the steps he took to maintain morale in the army with his orders of the day and his speeches to the assembled soldiers. His propaganda may be called a fourth kind of warfare, added to land, naval, and economic. Yet he recognized its limitations. "A good general, a good corps of officers, good organization, good training, rigid discipline make good troops, independent of the cause for which they fight." He discounted the value of speeches before a battle, saying the old soldiers did not listen and the recruits forgot them at the first cannon shot. Innuendo and false rumors should be destroyed, however, by the orders of the day.

In 1803 he organized the cavalry along lines that persisted as long as cavalry itself: light cavalry, dragoons, and heavy or battle cavalry. All these types were armed, and the cavalry had its own artillery. Napoléon's use of cavalry was masterful. In addition to the customary use for reconnaissance and pursuit, Napoléon employed it in all phases of battle. The cavalry screen was a new invention in 1805. The campaign of 1806 saw a new order of march, which Napoléon called the "squared battalion"; it was an attempt to approach the enemy by three parallel roads, with a cavalry screen across the entire front. Most of the cavalry was in independent units; Napoléon took the small formations of cavalry away from the divisions and united them into a corps. And he effected a co-ordination of the three major branches of the fighting forces: the infantry, the cavalry, and the artillery.

Several of Napoléon's most important military reforms concerned the artillery, at which he was expert. Even before Napoléon's day the artillery had interchangeable parts in the guns, carriages, and ammunition wagons. Napoléon standardized on a few gun calibers throughout the service. Formerly civilians had contracted to haul the guns to the battlefield, after which they had taken the horses away. This meant that the soldiers were forced to manhandle the guns if any moving was to be done during a battle. Napoléon eliminated this grievous system by including artillery horses on the regular table of supplies of the army. Auguste Marmont, who became one of Napoléon's marshals, was responsible for concentrating all the field guns under the division commander instead of scattering them throughout the battalions. Artillery was held in reserve at the disposal of the supreme commander.

Bonaparte was also the first to heed the admonition to have adequate reserves and use them intelligently. The formation of the Army of Reserve for the campaign of 1800 proved to be the decisive factor in defeating the Austrians, who could not believe that such an army actually existed.

Napoléon realized that war is not a science, but an art, "Nothing is absolute in war." For this reason Napoléon stated, "A general should say to himself many times a day: If the hostile army were to make its appearance on my front, on my right, or on my left, what should I do?" . . . "In everything that is undertaken, two thirds must be calculated and one third left to chance. To increase the first fraction would be pusillanimous; to augment the second would be rash." Himself an avid student of the campaigns of great captains, from Alexander [the Great] to Frederick [the Great of Prussia], Napoléon believed that "knowledge of grand tactics is gained only by experience and by the study of the history of the campaigns of all the great captains."

Yet warfare is based on principles and scientific knowledge. "All great captains have accomplished great things only by conforming to the rules and natural principles of the art of war." . . . "War should be made methodically, for it should have a definite object; and it should be conducted according to the principles and rules of the art. War should be made with forces proportionate to the obstacles which can be foreseen."

Being a successful general involved having certain personal qualities. Marshal Saxe said that the three basic qualities of a good general are courage, without which nothing else avails; intelligence, which should be courageous and "fertile in expedients"; and health. Napoléon's definition was strikingly similar:

> It is exceptional and difficult to find in one man all the qualities necessary for a great general. That which is most desirable and which instantly sets a man apart, is that his intelligence or talent be balanced by his character or courage. If his courage is the greater, a general heedlessly undertakes things beyond his ability. If on the contrary his character or courage is less than his intelligence he does not dare carry out his plans.

Napoléon shone particularly as a field commander. The

qualities that go to make up such a man are elusive; Napoléon thought a person was born with them. Among them are an ability to appraise the situation rapidly and accurately (for example, foreseeing developments merely by noting campfires on the eve of a battle); selecting exactly the right moment to take offensive action; understanding the psychology both of one's men and of the enemy commander. These items all fall under the rubric of military art rather than military science; if one could learn the clue to how he inspired his men, the effort put into the study would be well rewarded.

Napoléon Demonstrates His Ruthlessness

Owen Connelly

In the following excerpt from *Blundering to Glory: Napoléon's Military Campaigns*, Owen Connelly presents a young Napoléon who was given an opportunity to show whether or not he had the makings of a leader. A mob of about 80,000 Parisians was threatening the French Revolutionary government, and Napoléon was called in to command the forces that would guard the government at the Tuileries Palace. He quickly gathered all the cannons he could find from the surrounding areas and waited. Connelly describes how Napoléon ordered the cannons to be fired into the crowd at point-blank range. Many Parisians died, but, according to Connelly, Napoléon had shown himself to be an effective and ruthless commander. Napoléon's ambitious character was revealed not only in the battle, the author explains, but in how he manipulated his report of the event to increase his own political ends. Connelly is also the author of *The Epoch of Napoléon*.

In October 1795, the National Convention, sitting in the Tuileries Palace, came under threat of attack by the Paris mobs, irresistible since 1789. The Convention had written a new constitution creating the Directory, a moderate republican government. The Parisians were miserable. They blamed their plight on the Government of Thermidor, formed after the death of [French Revolution leader Maximilien de] Robespierre and named for the month of Thermidor in the Revolutionary Calendar, and they expected the new government to be no different. They still suffered from high unemployment, shortages of bread and fuel, and starvation and expo-

Excerpted from *Blundering to Glory: Napoléon's Military Campaigns,* by Owen Connelly. Copyright © 1990 by Scholarly Resources Inc. Reprinted by permission of Scholarly Resources Inc.

sure. Thousands were ready to march under the improbable leadership of royalists, who promised to take care of the people, and a few wealthy bourgeois who feared a return of the Terror.

[Paul] Barras was appointed to defend the Tuileries. He had once been an officer in the Royal Army, but for twenty years conquests of the boudoir and politics had occupied his time. He summoned Bonaparte to take actual command. He knew Napoléon from [Napoléon's first military victory at the Siege of] Toulon; he knew that he was ambitious and would ruthlessly use all his weapons. He also realized that if Bonaparte shocked the establishment, he was expendable; he was a foreigner and a loner, resented for his success in the officer corps.

Bonaparte found that artillery was his major need. He had 5,000 regular troops, some volunteers (the "Patriots of '89"), and a few gunners, but no cannon. He was certain that the infantry alone could not stand before 80,000 Parisians, an average mob when the people were aroused. Out of the swarm of officers in the foyer of the palace, Bonaparte therefore picked a tall Gascon cavalry major, Joachim Murat—a man he barely knew but who radiated force like his pawing stallion outside—and ordered him to take a troop of horsemen to Sablons, in the suburbs, and seize the cannon of the National Guard. As night fell, Murat led his men at a wild gallop through the narrow streets of Paris, scattering people, vehicles, and animals as he went. At Sablons, he spurred his horse through the gate with a final burst of speed, leaving guards standing agape; his men followed. Back through the streets he came in the early hours of the morning, bringing forty cannon, some pulled by artillery horses, others dragged by his cavalry with ropes.

NAPOLÉON FACES THE MOB

By dawn on 5 October, Napoléon had the guns emplaced to cover all approaches to the Tuileries, principally at the Rue de la Convention, which ran south from the Rue Saint-Honoré, then the "main street" of Paris, directly to the palace gardens. He had the guns charged with extra powder and loaded with canister (grapeshot) and, to make more shrapnel, nails, links of chain, and scrap metal.

All day the people gathered in increasing thousands along the Rue Saint-Honoré. They were hidden by densely packed buildings from the defenders of the Tuileries, who could only gauge the size of the crowd by the noise, which became ever louder. The people were building up their courage with the aid of free beer and wine furnished by their middle-class backers; their leaders were waiting for their numbers to become "irresistible."

At 4:00 P.M. the people could be seen forming ranks at the head of the Rue de la Convention. At 4:45 they came on, shouting the [French national anthem] *Marseillaise,* with pikes high, red liberty caps bobbing, in full confidence of victory. Napoléon's gunners, their cannon trained on the street, stood, torches lit, waiting for his command. They grew edgy as the mob moved in, first to 100 yards, then to 50 yards, and finally to point-blank range.

FIRE! The cannon cut bloody swaths through the crowd, and the people fled, leaving their dead and wounded among pools of blood on the cobblestones. The same scene, on a smaller scale, was enacted on the east side of the palace. It was all over. A few diehards held out in the church of Saint-Roch, but they were blasted out in short order. Napoléon disarmed the city.

NAPOLÉON'S POLITICAL GAIN

The Convention was saved. By grace of Bonaparte, the Directory became the government of the Republic. Four years later, by grace of the same general, it would fall and be replaced with a government of his own. At this point, however, his thoughts were far removed from being head of state. He sought promotion by pandering to Barras, the man who was de facto head of state and the only one of the five directors destined to serve for the whole life of the Directory. Accordingly, Napoléon's report credited General Barras with everything which had made victory possible, beginning with ordering the cannon brought from Sablons. Murat was not mentioned at all. (Not that Napoléon forgot him; he was later to be a marshal, the "First Horseman of Europe," husband of Napoléon's sister Caroline, Grand Duke of Berg, and King of Naples.) The report emphasized that the action had been defensive and called the attackers royalists, one and all. It made no mention of casualties but pointed out that among the dead were many émigré nobles, reactionary priests, and rebel guerrillas from the Vendée [western coastal region of France where counterrevolutionaries fought against the

French Revolution]. Privately, Napoléon wrote [his brother] Joseph that his gunners had killed *"beaucoup de monde"*— uncounted numbers of the attackers.

Apparently he was afraid he might be accused of excessive brutality, but he need not have worried. As he wrote Joseph on 11 October: "We were victorious, and all is forgotten." Parisians were quiet, if hardly in love with Bonaparte. The republican establishment was jubilant; the officer corps accepted the politicians' opinion. Napoléon was promoted to major general and given command of the Army of the Interior. In March 1796 he was made general-in-chief of the Army of Italy, which he soon led to victories that made him world famous.

A Quest for Personal Glory

Jean Tulard

In the following reading from *Napoléon: The Myth of the Saviour*, author Jean Tulard describes Napoléon's Egyptian campaign as more of an attempt to achieve personal glory than a military campaign to benefit France. According to Tulard, Napoléon needed a well-publicized victory in order to win the hearts of the people enough to promote himself into higher political office. Although Napoléon's military operations in Egypt were a disaster, the scientific, economic, and intellectual expeditions he sponsored were very successful. Tulard explains how Napoléon's propaganda made him a hero despite his considerable losses, paving the way for his ascension to power.

During a journey from 8–20 February 1798, Napoléon Bonaparte had taken into account the difficulties which the [proposed French] plan to invade England presented. He risked losing all his prestige in an expedition where General Lazare Hoche had already failed. In the report which he addressed to the Directory on 23 February he observed:

> Whatever our efforts, we will not acquire naval supremacy in a few years. To undertake an invasion of England without being lords of the sea would be the boldest and most difficult operation ever carried out. It would require the long nights of winter. After the month of April it would be impossible to undertake anything.

He suggested two other solutions: to attack Hanover [Germany], or to conquer Egypt—a plan which had been developed by [Charles Maurice de] Talleyrand, the Foreign Minister. The first solution was reasonable—too much so for Bonaparte's thirst for glory, equally too much so for the Directory, which was eager to be rid, as soon as possible, of an

Excerpted from *Napoléon: The Myth of the Saviour*, by Jean Tulard, translated by Teresa Waugh. Copyright © Librarie Arthème Fayard 1977; English translation © George Weidenfeld & Nicolson Ltd. 1984. Reprinted by permission of Weidenfeld & Nicolson Ltd.

embarrassing general. The conquest of Egypt seemed madness. It meant depriving France of an army, and of an experienced general, at a time when war threatened to break out at any moment on the Continent; it meant attempting to escape the British fleet in the Mediterranean, and attacking a country which was as yet little known despite the insistence of [Charles] Magallon, the French Consul in Cairo, on the simplicity of such a conquest. But the East caught Bonaparte's imagination; furthermore, the whole operation allowed him to leave the political situation in France to rot in his absence. Public opinion, on learning of the plan, was very enthusiastic for an expedition to a mysterious land made fashionable by [French historian and philosopher Constantin-François de Chaseboef, Comte de] Volney in *Les Ruines* [The Ruins]. Finally the Directory saw, without displeasure, the removal of a formidable menace.

WHY NAPOLÉON INVADED EGYPT

Egypt presented a triple interest; it made it possible in the immediate future, by occupying the isthmus of Suez, to cut off one of the trade routes from India to England; destined to become a colony, 'she would alone,' said Talleyrand, 'be worth all those that France had lost'; she would then provide a useful base for the future conquest of Britain's principal source of wealth—India, where [Sultan] Tipu Sahib was leading the fight against the British invasion.

The Eastern expedition combined scientific interest with military and economic objectives. It followed a long line of eighteenth-century voyages of discovery. A committee for the sciences and the arts was to accompany the army and to found an Egyptian Institute. . . . Twenty-one mathematicians, three astronomers, seventeen civil engineers, thirteen naturalists and mining engineers, as many geographers, three gunpowder and saltpetre experts, four architects, eight draftsmen, ten mechanical draftsmen, one sculptor, fifteen interpreters, ten writers and twenty-two printers bearing Roman, Greek and Arabic characters, made the journey. . . .

By giving a scientific character to his expedition, Bonaparte confirmed his alliance with the ideologues. In the final analysis the conquest of Egypt seemed to be, above all, an exercise of internal politics: Bonaparte was too much of a realist, despite the declarations attributed to him, to consider, like Alexander [the Great, Greek monarch], carving out an

Napoléon leads the charge toward the conquest of Egypt. Along with military and economic objectives, Egypt was considered easy prey to increase Napoléon's glory.

Eastern empire. Starting with religion and language, there were too many obstacles in his path. It is undeniable that afterwards he envisaged dividing the Ottoman [Empire, a Muslim power that controlled southeastern Europe, the Middle East, and North Africa] possessions with the [Russian] Tsar [Alexander I], and that he later dreamed of an Egypt reborn under the French administration, and even of a Universal Empire. But in 1798 he was thinking, above all, of going away in order to avoid compromising the prestige he had acquired. Once the Mediterranean was crossed, Egypt seemed an easy prey. Bonaparte hoped by his victory to increase his glory whilst the government in Paris continued to disintegrate. He admitted it: he was aiming at France whilst awaiting Europe. When and how? He did not know as yet. But one can be sure that he did not think of shutting himself away in Egypt.

THE ATTACK ON EGYPT

On 19 May two hundred ships under the command of Admiral [François-Paul] Brueys and carrying thirty-five thousand men, left Toulon.

Everything had been prepared within a month: soldiers, materials and ships—which is evidence of Bonaparte's impatience to leave Paris, temporarily of course; it also explains the inevitable gaps which soon appeared in the material preparations for the expedition. These preparations had not escaped the notice of the British Admiralty, but [Lord Horatio] Nelson missed the French fleet twice and thought there must have been an intervention in Turkey. Meanwhile, in passing, Bonaparte took Malta without firing a shot. On 1 July he landed without resistance in the Bay of Alexandria. The town soon fell into French hands. But the army's enthusiasm disappeared at an early stage when confronted by the desert, the filth, the poverty and the heat. (Bonaparte had chosen the season very badly and appears never to have taken meteorological considerations into account when planning his campaigns.) According to an eye-witness, Bricard, 'Our soldiers were dying in the sand from lack of water and food; an excessive heat had forced them to jettison their spoils, and some, weary of suffering, had blown out their brains.' Many, despite the reading of a proclamation, were querying the reason for having come to such a hostile land. François Bernoyer, chief of supplies to the Army of the Orient, wrote to his wife:

> I have made inquiries into what our government anticipated when it sent an army to occupy the Sultan's States without any declaration of war and with no motive for declaring it. A little sagacity is all that is needed, I have been told. Bonaparte, by virtue of his genius and victories won with an army which had become invincible, had too great an influence in France. He was an embarrassment not to say an obstacle to those who hold the reins of power. I was able to discover no other causes.

That says all that need be said about the morale of the Army of the Orient.

As a province of the Ottoman Empire, Egypt was in fact subject to the military feudal system of the Mamelukes, originally slaves bought from among the populations of the Caucasus [Russia and Central Asia]. This warlike caste ruled over a people consisting of small artisans, tradespeople and fellahin [Egyptian peasants], all of whom were increasingly dissatisfied with their rulers, particularly since Egypt at the end of the eighteenth century was suffering from a marked economic slump. The warnings of the Consul Magallon were confirmed by the rapid collapse of the Mamelukes. One battle was enough: it took place at Giza, opposite Cairo, near the great pyramids, on 21 July. The Mameluke cavalry charges dashed themselves against the French infantry squares. The victory, which has become legendary, has been grossly exaggerated. It did at least ensure Bonaparte's possession of Cairo.

Napoléon Encounters Reversals

But on 1 August the French fleet which had escaped the British ships during the crossing was surprised by Nelson in Aboukir Bay and entirely destroyed. Bonaparte was a prisoner of his own victory.

The situation worsened with Turkey's declaration of war in September and the threat of an intervention by Ottoman forces. Sickness due to the climate also had to be taken into account. The hostility of the inhabitants was made apparent in the revolt of Cairo on 21 October which cost the lives of General Dupuy and of Bonaparte's favourite aide-de-camp, [Joseph] Sulkowski. This terrible insurrection revealed the extent of the Muslim leaders' forces.

Nevertheless everything was done to win the sympathy of the population. Religious beliefs were respected, the old feudal system was destroyed, the canals were rehabilitated, the economy was boosted. The levelling of the Suez isthmus and the works preparatory to the joining of the Red Sea and the Mediterranean were started under the direction of the chief engineer, Le Père. An Egyptian Institute, modelled on the Institut de France was founded. Its objective was 'progress and the spreading of enlightenment in Egypt'. Two newspapers were published in French: *Le Courrier de L'Égypte* and *La Décade égyptienne*. There was a re-launching of an Egypt freed from the economic and social, if not religious, restraints imposed by the Mameluke rule. The past was not forgotten: excavations at Thebes, Luxor and Karnak; the discovery of the Rosetta Stone [ancient Egyptian stone whose deciphering resulted in the understanding of hieroglyphics] as well as numerous sketches by Vivant Denon and his team of artists comprised the main elements of a fruitful harvest which was to lead to the publication, from 1809, of the great volumes of the *Description d'Égypte.*

War continued. The Turks were in fact marching on Egypt: Bonaparte went to meet them in Syria in February 1799. This expedition was carefully prepared. Gaza (where two thousand Turks were massacred), and then Jaffa, fell without difficulty. But the French were to fail at Saint-Jean-d'Acre which was defended by Pasha Djezzar and a former fellow-student of Bonaparte's, Phélippeaux. The town had been supplied with fresh provisions by Commander Sidney Smith's British fleet, while, on the other hand, the French troops were short of siege artillery. In his letters, Bernoyer asserts that some generals, . . . worried by plans attributed to Bonaparte—such as that of having himself crowned King of Persia—'did everything to prevent the taking of Saint-Jean-d'Acre'. Sickness played its part. Besides, a Turkish army advancing from Damas had to be stopped near Nazareth on 16 April with the Battle of Mount Tabor. Another army which had landed at Aboukir on 25 July was crushed by Bonaparte who had hurried back to Egypt. Before that, Lanusse had crushed an uprising stirred up by El Modhy.

NAPOLÉON RETURNS TO FRANCE

The oriental dream was becoming a nightmare—more especially as the news from Paris was bad. A lack of precise information led to the spreading of the most fantastic rumours. The naval disaster at Aboukir and the Cairo revolt were blown up by Bonaparte's adversaries; Bonaparte, cut off from France, lacking communications, had difficulty in reacting. The English were interfering and exposing Bonaparte's atrocities. They complacently described the massacre of French soldiers, overtaken by the plague, or of defenceless Turks. Bonapartist propaganda was spineless and found it hard to make a 'deportation of the general and the élite of the Army of Italy' sound credible. With the renewal of war on the Continent, public attention was turned to other battlefields. There was rumour of a *coup d'état* prepared by [French politician Emmanuel] Sieyès with the agreement of a brilliant general, [Barthélemy] Joubert. Bonaparte's absence was turning against him. On 26 August, [Jean-Baptiste] Kléber, who had been made Commander-in-Chief of the Army of Egypt, informed the troops of the departure of their general on the 23rd. The message left by the General himself explained this desertion as follows: 'Extraordinary circumstances alone have persuaded me, in the interests of my country, its glory, and of obedience, to pass through enemy lines and to return to Europe.'. . . He was taking a double risk: the British surveillance of the Mediterranean had to be avoided; and even though Bonaparte was ordered back officially on 26 May, he would still have to justify his departure. There were two miracles: the ship was not intercepted; and the report of the victory at Aboukir on 24 July arrived in Paris several days before Bonaparte. It gave the lie to the pessimistic rumours about the Army of Egypt, which had been rife up till then and it impressed the public with an account of Bonaparte's brilliant victory. It was forgotten that the Army of the Orient had reached an impasse and that its absence had weighed heavily in the first setbacks of the new Continental war. So Bonaparte had been right to distance himself from the Directory. In spite of the failures of the Egyptian expedition he returned to France in an aura of prestige won by far-off victories which had been exaggerated by the propaganda of his partisans. Joubert had been bribed, [French general Jean] Moreau was too compromised, [French marshal Jean Baptiste Jules] Bernadotte too prudent. The way was open. So the 'saviour in boots', called upon to end the Revolution and heralded by [French Revolution leader Maximilien de] Robespierre in 1792 when he denounced the belligerent politics of the Girondins [French Revolution political group], was to be Bonaparte.

Napoléon's Masterpiece: The Battle of Austerlitz

David G. Chandler

David G. Chandler, former deputy head of the Department of War Studies at the Royal Military Academy Sandhurst, England, is chair in Military Studies at the U.S. Marine Corps University. The following reading is from his book *On the Napoléonic Wars: Collected Essays*. Chandler describes the 1805 battle at Austerlitz (located in the former Czech Republic) as Napoléon's masterpiece of military strategy. Facing the Third Coalition—the alliance of Great Britain, Russia, Sweden, and Austria—Napoléon's 68,000 troops soundly defeated the larger force of 90,000 Russians and Austrians. Chandler explains that Napoléon's ability to inspire his soldiers and his use of speedy attacks, courageous bluffing, and superior mobility confirmed Napoléon's reputation as a great military commander. Chandler has published extensively on Napoléon, including *The Campaigns of Napoléon, Napoléon, A Dictionary of the Napoléonic Wars, Waterloo: The Hundred Days, The Military Maxims of Napoléon*, and *Austerlitz*.

The battle of Austerlitz takes its name from a medium-sized town (now known as Slavkov) in Moravia (today part of the [former] Czech Republic). Four miles west of the township are the Pratzen Heights, in 1805 the centre of a mighty battle fought by 158,000 men equipped with 417 cannon—36,000 of whom would become casualties before dark on that freezing December day. Exactly one year earlier Napoléon had crowned himself Emperor at Notre Dame—as his soldiers now reminded him, shouting 'c'est l'anniversaire' [it's the anniversary] and forming an impromptu torchlight procession as he strolled through their bivouacs in the dark early hours of that fateful Monday morning. Deeply touched by this evidence of his soldiers' loyalty and affection, he could find no words to thank them but slowly moved his hand to and fro in recognition of their spontaneous demonstration. 'This has been the finest evening of my life,' he was heard to murmur as he lay back to snatch a few hours rest in his straw-floored tent. But an even finer one lay close ahead. Before sunset that same day he would have established his place in history as one of the truly 'great captains' of all time. For Napoléon personally, Austerlitz would forever afterwards rank as his favourite battle. It was destined to be his masterpiece of operational art—of battlefield command.

WHY THE BATTLE WAS FOUGHT

The origins of the War of the Third Coalition [Great Britain, Russia, Sweden, Austria] go back to the seizure on neutral soil and subsequent hasty execution of the Bourbon prince, the Duke of Enghien in March 1804. This ruthless deed—intended to serve as a warning to would-be assassins—caused a storm of European outrage, creating a Francophobic atmosphere that British premier William Pitt the Younger hastened to exploit. As Napoléon's ruthless Minister of Police, Joseph Fouché, trenchantly remarked, 'It was more than a crime—it was a mistake.' Napoléon further eased the task of his inveterate British foe by next crowning himself Emperor in late 1804 and then King of Italy (May 1805). These political acts, added to the 'judicial murder' of the Bourbon royal princeling, inalienably affronted the ancient royal houses of Europe. The Habsburg Emperor Francis II [Austrian] in Vienna and the Romanov Tsar Alexander I [of Russia] in St Petersburg—the two crowned heads who would share with Napoléon the events of 2 December 1805—proceeded to negotiate alliances with Great Britain, and were joined by Sweden, Naples and other Germanic states to put a joint 400,000 men into the field against France. A decidedly complex seven-part strategic plan evolved, but so shoddy was the staff work of the Allies of the Third Coalition that Vienna even failed to realise the twelve-day difference between the west European and Russian calendars. . . .

The main secrets of Napoléon's success to date were surprise, the seizure and keeping of the initiative, and the superb mobility and flexibility that the army corps system conferred.

Each corps was in effect a miniature army, 17,000 to 30,000 men strong. It was a balanced, all-arms, self-sufficient formation, capable of operating alone (thus easing road problems and facilitating 'living off the countryside') and, if necessary, of fighting a far superior force for up to twenty-four hours. Napoléon placed his corps in a flexible strategic net, capable of rapidly reinforcing any threatened sector by 'marching on the sound of the guns'. 'March dispersed, fight concentrated' was another key Napoléonic maxim. This system had been tried out before, but only now in 1805 was its full potential being demonstrated. Small wonder that Napoléon's foot-sore soldiers remarked: 'The Emperor has discovered a new way of making war: he makes use of our legs instead of our arms.'. . .

NAPOLÉON'S BATTLE PLAN

With the far stronger Allied army only forty miles away, Napoléon was in an increasingly precarious position. So at least thought the bright sparks around the Tsar, who were strongly supported by the Austrian General [Franz von] Weyrother, 'a veteran of the Viennese offices' (or military bureaucrat). These pressure groups demanded an immediate counter-offensive. Francis II and [Russian army commander Prince Mikhail Illarionovich] Kutusov advised caution, only to be contemptuously scorned and ignored by the firebrands, who included the twenty-eight-year-old Alexander.

Napoléon was well aware of the peril—but determined to turn it to his own advantage. To redress part of his manpower shortfall, he summoned by forced marches I Corps from Iglau (mercifully there were still no firm signs of Prussia entering the war), and also [French general Louis-Nicolas, duke of Auerstadt] Davout's III Corps from Vienna all of eighty miles distant, creating a dense cavalry screen to mask these vital transfers. Meanwhile, the French deliberately gave every appearance of irresolution further to fool the Allies. Cavalry outposts were ordered to fall back from near Wischau, Austerlitz was evacuated, and even the dominating high ground of the Pratzen Heights abandoned—all in order to create an impression of French weakness and low morale. Napoléon next switched his lines of communication from the dangerously exposed highroad to Vienna to that running west towards Iglau.

He began to feign weakness, requesting an armistice and

peace negotiations (both were brusquely refused), and step by step he set about inducing the Russo-Austrian high command to attack his exposed right (which the foe was induced to consider but weakly held, although Davout's secret arrival in the area would swing the balance) and the road to Vienna beyond it. As early as 21 November he had required his staff to study the area west of the Goldbach stream: 'Gentlemen, examine this ground carefully. It is going to be a battlefield: you will have a part to play upon it.'

On 1 December it was clear that the Allies were duly falling for the bait dangled so temptingly before their eyes, blinded as they were by the prospect of an easy and decisive victory. After a two-day advance along the Olmütz to Brünn road, most Allied divisions swung off to the south to occupy the undefended Pratzen area ready to envelop Napoléon's right wing and thus cut him off from Vienna. Their commanders and staffs met at Krzenowitz late on 1 December. Little did they realise that before nightfall the French strength had been raised to over 66,000 men following [French general Jean Baptiste Jules] Bernadotte's unostentatious arrival from the west, or that 6,600 more reinforcements under Davout's command were near Raigern Abbey after a heroic march of eighty miles from Vienna in just fifty hours. As news reached Napoléon that masses of the enemy were collecting on and to the south of the Pratzen Heights, his confidence grew. 'Before tomorrow evening this army will be mine!' he prophesied. '*On les aura!*' ('We shall have them!'). . . .

Napoléon's plan was to lure the foe into making a heavy attack against his apparently weak right flank, which would, however, be reinforced at the critical moment by Davout's nearby formations. . . . Once the mass of the enemy was committed to these attacks, Napoléon intended to launch [French military commander Nicolas-Jean de Dieu] Soult's two concealed divisions from the valley floor against Pratzen village and its surrounding heights, and thus occupy the denuded enemy centre. Reinforced by Bernadotte and the Guard, Soult would then roll up either the enemy left or right according to the prevailing circumstances. The various corps were to be linked by visual telegraph—a line of inter-visible flag stations—once the fog lifted. To put his men on their mettle, a flamboyant order of the day was issued.

That he had divined his opponents' intentions was indicated by the campfires burning to the southward and the fierce skirmishing around Telnitz about midnight. Napoléon and his escort rode over to observe, and almost ran into a patrol of Cossacks, but safely returned to the French lines. Napoléon then walked through his cheering army. By 2.30 A.M., all was quiet once more. . . .

THE FINAL BATTLE

Napoléon was roused once from his sleep to approve a minor change to strengthen the French right. And so the scene was at last set for Napoléon's greatest battle. A final briefing of senior officers was held atop the Zurlan at 5.30 A.M. Concern that [French general Jean] Lannes would come to blows with Soult over a misunderstanding of several days' standing proved unnecessary. 'We have more serious things to engage our attention,' Soult loftily informed the fire-spitting Gascon [Lannes]—who growlingly concurred and stood aside. The last orders given, all save Soult and [Napoléon's chief of staff Louis Alexandre] Berthier departed to their prescribed battle stations. . . .

THE AFTERMATH

By 4.30 P.M. the last shots had been fired. Napoléon, accompanied by Berthier and Soult, rode slowly down to the valley, and then northwards, to the plaudits of his troops. The cost of victory had not been slight; more than 9,000 Frenchmen had become casualties (12 per cent of the whole). Inevitably, the Allies had fared far worse. Besides their captives, another 15,000 were dead or seriously wounded (or some 32 per cent).

There was no immediate pursuit—both sides were equally exhausted. As he rode towards the post-house of Posoritz, where he would spend the night, Napoléon repeatedly paused to organise succour for the wounded. On his orders, his escort stripped greatcoats from the Russian dead to lay them over the wounded. Sometimes it was noted that the Emperor dispensed brandy with his own hand. Arrived at his lodging, he took a simple supper before starting to write a short note to Josephine: 'I have beaten the Austro-Russian army commanded by the two Emperors. I am a little weary. I have camped in the open for eight days and as many freezing nights. Tomorrow I shall be able to rest in the castle of Prince [Wenzel Anton von] Kaunitz, and I should be able to snatch two or three hours sleep there. The Russian army is not only beaten but destroyed. I embrace you. Napoléon.' Taking a second sheet of paper he began to write the Order of the Day: 'Soldiers! I am content with you . . .', he began. But then weariness overwhelmed him. Next morning the pursuit of the shattered Allies commenced. . . . Meanwhile, Napoléon's

A STIMULANT FOR NAPOLÉON'S AMBITION

The Battle of Austerlitz was Napoléon's greatest military victory, not only because it significantly extended the French Empire, but also because of the strategic brilliance demonstrated by Napoléon. In this passage from The Battle of Austerlitz: Napoléon's Greatest Victory, *author Trevor N. Depuy shows the influence this victorious battle had on Napoléon's career and ambitions.*

Not the least of the consequences of Austerlitz was its effect on Napoléon's own career. He could rightly look upon it as the perfect battle, a masterpiece of foresight, intuition, and care for detail, one which he executed as brilliantly as he had planned it. Napoléon was too intelligent ever to believe that the exact circumstances of that battle could be re-created. And many times in later years he was to demonstrate the same matchless skill which had won that battle. But the ease with which he had won the battle and the results it achieved for him led the emperor to half-believe the fawning courtiers who told him he was invincible. Even to the end of his career he felt that, if need be, he could always create another Austerlitz.

Furthermore, the great victory whetted his already great ambition and caused him to have less concern for the rights and privileges of other people. As a young officer fighting for the Revolution, Napoléon had opposed the tyranny of the French kings. But now he began to use methods just as ruthless, and just as tyrannical, to further his ambition to become the most powerful man in the world. He became more interested in using the ideals of the French Revolution to make enemy rulers unpopular than he was in trying to improve the living conditions of the common people. And though his efficient government had made France prosperous, his wars were destined to undo much of his good work, and to bring sorrow, misery, and hardship to most of the French people. They would bring Napoléon himself to defeat and ruin in Russia and at Waterloo.

Trevor N. Dupuy, *The Battle of Austerlitz: Napoléon's Greatest Victory,* 1968.

completed communiqué lavished praise on his men, and distributed favours and monetary rewards wholesale.

The results of Austerlitz were impressive in both military and political terms. There was no further thought of the Allies continuing the struggle. Two days later an open-air interview took place between Napoléon and the Emperor Francis at the latter's request. It was agreed that an armistice would come into immediate effect, and that peace talks would begin at Vienna. These resulted in the Peace of Pressburg, signed on 26 December. By its terms, Venice was added to the Kingdom of Italy, and Istria, Croatia and Dalmatia ceded to France, Swabia was awarded to Württemberg, and the Tyrol, Vorarlberg and other Alpine enclaves given to Bavaria. Thus the two loyal French Germanic confederates received their rewards. Meanwhile the Russians continued eastwards. Davout's hard-marching columns caught up with the Russians at Göding, and renewed hostilities appeared imminent. But the Tsar and Kutusov claimed that they had already concluded an armistice—in fact this was not the case, but Davout chose to accept their declarations at face value. Observed by [French general] Savary, chief of intelligence, the Russians comprised '. . . no more than 26,000 . . . all arms included. Most of them had lost their knapsacks, and a great number were wounded but they marched bravely in the ranks.' The Tsar sent Davout and Savary a message for transmission to Napoléon. 'Tell your master that I am going away. Tell him that he has performed miracles . . . that the battle has increased my admiration for him; that he is a man predestined by Heaven; that it will require a hundred years for my army to equal his.'

When news of Austerlitz reached England, it proved the last blow for the ailing William Pitt, who would die in January 1806. Shortly before the end, he told his niece, Hester Stanhope: 'Roll up that map of Europe. It will not be wanted these ten years.' As for Napoléon, he was now well on the way to becoming master of Europe.

THE IMPORTANCE OF AUSTERLITZ

For the rest of his life Napoléon drew pleasure from recollecting the battle of Austerlitz and its surrounding events. When, in 1808, consideration was being given to suitable ducal titles for award to the Marshalate, Soult suggested that his might be 'Duke of Austerlitz'. The idea was abruptly re-

jected; Davout might be created Duke of Auerstädt. . . .
Austerlitz was one title that Napoléon was determined not to
award—but keep for himself.

Why did the Emperor accord the battle such priority? Why
did he deem Austerlitz more important than, say, [his victories at] Rivoli, Friedland or Wagram? In the first place it was
the first full trial-of-strength since the creation of the Empire,
and the refinement of France's soldiery into the unified Grand
Army. It is sometimes overlooked that this was Napoléon's
first major campaign, and great battle, for five-and-a-half
years. Not since Marengo (14 June 1800) had he been in a
major engagement (if we exclude Ulm, which was a special
case). It represented, therefore, the full testing of his martial
skills and genius—and the result had been triumph. After
Austerlitz, Napoléon's reputation as a great commander—
first gained in 1796—had received confirmation.

The plan of campaign—rapidly extemporised in August
1805 to meet the new challenge posed by the Third Coalition—had illustrated Napoléon's mastery of strategy. Appreciating the chance to catch [Austrian general Charles] Mack's
and [Italian archduke and Austrian army commander] Fer-
dinand's Austrians on their own, he had moved 210,000 men
in a bold sweep through central Europe. Not every detail had
been foreseen—the anticipated battle on the River Iller had
never materialised, for instance—but Napoléon's strategic
system had proved flexible enough to adjust to circumstances. Nor had the subsequent pursuit of the retreating Kutusov been as successful as hoped. It was not Napoléon's
wish to see the Russians able to rendezvous with their second army at Wischau, nor to be drawn in his turn ever
deeper into Moravia in search of a decisive battle in the very
depth of a bitter winter. His remaining men—when the effects of strategic consumption had been taken into account—
were exhausted, tattered and nigh-starving. But the carefully
planned web of army corps still permitted Napoléon substantially to redress the numerical imbalance on the eve—
and even the very day—of battle. Here indeed was the hand
of a great master of war at work. He took huge risks, but they
were calculated ones.

Using his actual weakness to delude his superior opponents, Napoléon had then excelled in imposing his wishes
upon them at the operational level. To produce substantial
reserves was one thing; to induce the enemy into adopting

the battle-plan that best suited the French, quite another. True, not every detail of the bitter day's fighting was foreseen in advance: 'one engages, and then one sees'—a maxim that was very much illustrated by the touch-and-go and critical battle for retention of the Pratzen Heights between 10 A.M. and midday. 'There is a moment in engagements when the least manoeuvre is decisive and gives a victory,' runs another Napoléonic maxim; 'It is the one drop of water which causes the vessel to run over'—in this case probably the decision of General [Paul-Charles Heri] Thiébault to order his wavering brigade to charge [the] masses rather than retire. Battle control of a very high order had then been needed to overcome the crisis in the centre as the Russian Imperial Guard attacked. And it was only at about 2.30 P.M. that Napoléon made up his mind which wing of the staggering but still powerful Allied army to envelop: once again, essentially an extemporised decision.

But successful extemporisation is one necessary aspect of a demonstrable genius for waging war, just as 'an infinite capacity for taking pains' is another, and an ability to inspire soldiers at times of great peril, a third. Above all, perhaps, the determination to fight a fluid battle, one of continual movement, lay behind the great success. The key, as the percipient General Savary wrote later, '. . . was that we moved about a great deal, and that individual divisions fought successive actions on different parts of the field. This is what multiplied our forces throughout the day, and this is what the art of warfare is all about . . .' These gifts—and many more—Napoléon had demonstrated at many levels during 1805. Small wonder that an important boulevard in Paris is named after the battle, or that the main training area at St Cyr-Coëtiquidian is named 'the Pratzen', where each 2 December a large re-enactment of Austerlitz is performed by all the French officer-cadets under training before a select audience of staff and guests. For Austerlitz had once and for all set the seal on the creation of the French Empire and upon Napoléon's reputation as a soldier of preeminent ability. Such has been posterity's verdict. Austerlitz had proved one of the greatest battles in modern military history.

Napoléon Overreaches in Russia

Anthony Masters

Anthony Masters describes Napoléon's three-month march to Moscow which culminated in a battle that killed over 74,000 soldiers. Napoléon's victory was hollow, however, he claims. Although the French occupied Moscow, the Russians never sued for peace and refused to engage the French army in battle. He also points out that the decisions Napoléon made during the Russian campaign illustrate how he was well past his prime as a military strategist. Masters is the author of *Napoléon*.

Napoléon decided on a wholesale invasion of Russia with an army of half a million men. "What a man!" said his friend the Count of Narbonne, dazed after an imperial interview. "What tremendous ideas! What dreams! He's a genius, but is he all right in the head?" When Denis, Duc de Decrès, one of Napoléon's admirals, was asked if the Emperor would make a Russian city his capital, he replied bitterly, "He will not long have any capital; he will not return from this war; or if he returns, it will be without his army." Those around Napoléon noticed that his razor-sharp judgment seemed strangely blunted. His health, too, had deteriorated. He had become very fat and had perpetual stomach pains.

THE MARCH TO MOSCOW

Still, his heart was set on Russia. "These barbarians," he said, "must be driven back into their own ice, so that for the next 25 years they won't come and interfere with civilized Europe." Despite having an army of 450,000 men, he planned an operation that would only have been practicable in a smaller country with a smaller force. They crossed the river Niemen, which formed the boundary between Prussia and Russia, on

June 24th, 1812. That day, a hare suddenly darted up between the legs of Napoléon's horse, causing it to swerve and throw him. He tried to laugh it off, but his touchiness showed that, like everyone else, he recognized it as a bad omen.

Men and horses were soon very short of food. It is now believed that about three quarters of Napoléon's army died, some in battle but most of starvation, before they even saw Moscow. The 800-kilometer journey to the capital began to seem an impossible task. They pressed on, the Emperor vaguely hoping for an opportunity to face the much smaller Russian army in battle, smash them and bring the campaign to a swift conclusion. But the Russians were not so foolish. As the Tsar [Alexander I] had written a year earlier, "The system which has made [British military leader, Duke of] Wellington victorious [in Spain], and exhausted the French armies, is what I am resolved to follow—avoid pitched battles. . ." The Tsar's ambassador in London foresaw events with incredible precision: "We can win by persistent defense and retreat. If the enemy begins to pursue us, it is all up with him; for the further he advances from his bases of supply and munitions into a trackless and foodless country, starved and encircled by an army of Cossacks, his position will become more and more dangerous; and he will end by being destroyed by the winter, which has always been our most faithful ally."

The march to Moscow took almost three months. It was only at the very end that the French caught up with the Russians outside Moscow, at Borodino, where they had dug themselves in. Napoléon's army was now reduced to half its number, and it had not yet fought a battle. Its task was made more difficult by the position of the Russian army, beside the Moskva river, on high ground with its center protected by a formidable display of artillery. Napoléon knew his losses would be heavy. In the battle, which began on September 7th, 1812, 600 French and 600 Russian guns pounded each other all day; 30,000 French and 44,000 Russians died. Both armies were broken, but, since it was the Russians who retreated, Napoléon could claim it as a victory. Years later, however, he recalled it as "the most terrible of all my battles. . . . The French showed themselves worthy of victory, and the Russians worthy of being invincible." That mighty deadlock was itself an achievement of which the Russians could justifiably be proud.

NAPOLÉON TAKES MOSCOW

But the way to Moscow was open, and a week later Napoléon entered it with the 130,000 soldiers who survived. To their amazement, they found the city totally deserted and silent. The entire population had abandoned it to the invaders. Un-

Napoléon and his forces are shown retreating from a disastrous winter invasion of Russia. The French army was ravaged by cold and starvation.

deterred, Napoléon occupied the Tsar's apartments in the Kremlin. But that night, one of his valets awoke in the small hours, to find that a glow in the sky was lighting up his bedroom. He looked out of the window, and saw that he was in the middle of a burning city.

The Russians had started fires throughout the city, after first immobilizing the fire engines. An incendiary fuse was even found in the imperial bedroom of the Kremlin. Strong winds made it impossible to prevent the fire from spreading. The stables, housing some of Napoléon's own horses, were saved by men working, as an eyewitness put it, "beneath a vault of fire." But whole districts of the city were completely destroyed.

After the fire was finally extinguished, the French stayed two weeks, while Napoléon waited for the Tsar to make peace. But no message came. Napoléon could not understand it. He could have forced the Tsar's hand by marching on St. Petersburg, but the problems of maintaining discipline and preventing desertion on such a long trek were enough to deter him. So the French waited at Moscow, for a month in all.

WINTER RAVAGES THE FRENCH ARMY

That month turned out to be crucial. Typically, Napoléon was so convinced that the Tsar had to come to terms that he never considered what the consequences would be if he did not. He never thought of the Russian winter and scornfully dismissed the warnings of his aide, General Armand de Caulaincourt, that a retreat in November and December could have terrible consequences. The weather itself, which remained mild long after autumn should have begun, helped to lull him into a false sense of security. Finally, a little snow fell, then a good deal of rain. Napoléon decided to abandon Moscow and retrace his steps a little way, in the hope of meeting and annihilating the Russian army and replenishing stores from stocks at Smolensk, which might well be the best place to spend the winter. (The route went past Bordino, where the corpses of the victims, still there after seven weeks, presented a grisly spectacle.) At Smolensk, which they reached on 9th November, came the appalling realization that the stores were far too depleted to be of much use. The starving men grabbed what there was. It was clear that they would have to push on. Now winter began to set in. "It seemed as if the Emperor were expecting some miracle to alter the climate," noted de Caulaincourt. The horses, which were not shod for travelling on ice (de Caulaincourt, without telling Napoléon, had done that for the imperial household horses and so ensured their survival), fell and were left to die, or were cut up for food while they were still alive. Again, men began to die of starvation, and the news that Minsk, which

HARDSHIP IN RUSSIA

On September 15, 1812, Napoléon entered Moscow in triumph after soundly defeating the Russian army. However, an unexpectedly early winter left Napoléon's Grande Armée without food or supplies. The following passage by a German soldier serving under Napoléon shows just how devastating the winter was for the common soldier.

On the 24th I was entrusted with the odd and, under the prevailing conditions, preposterous mission of assembling all the stray chasseurs; wandering along the road and re-forming them into a fighting unit. Being on foot I had some success by day in gathering and keeping together a few of them, but as soon as night fell and we had to look for sleeping quarters they discovered that I had not so much as a bite of food or anything else to offer them. So away they melted again. Though I realized that I would receive a reprimand if I should happen to meet my commanding officer next day without my retinue, I neither could nor would make even an attempt to force these famished men to stay with me by putting them under formal orders.

The night of the 24th to the 25th I found a barn filled with hay into which I dug myself deep to escape the cold. The next night I spent in a wood, out in the open in the snow, without so much as a fire, and had I not pulled myself together every now and again to walk up and down and keep my circulation going I would undoubtedly have frozen to death. . . .

When I left Smolensk I had provisions for no more than one day, that is to say, a small bag of flour. By the next day I was already reduced to eating horse flesh and though, from time to time, I did come upon something more palatable it was usually no more than scraps offered me out of kindness by people who had little enough to spare. Never was it enough to still the pangs of hunger. Even of the revolting horse flesh there was never enough to go round.

H.A. Vossler, "The Retreat of Napoléon's Grande Armée from Russia," in *The Mammoth Book of Eye-Witness History*, Jon E. Lewis, ed., 1998.

might have provided stores, had fallen into Russian hands was a terrible blow. Boots wore out, exposing bare feet to frostbite. Soon, Napoléon's men were dying of cold, but still they did not forget to spare some firewood, when they had any, to warm their beloved Emperor. He, meanwhile, was looked after well, riding in a carriage drawn by his properly shod horses and provided with good meat and bread, his favorite vegetables (beans and lentils), and his favorite kind of Burgundy wine.

Gradually the great army was whittled away to almost nothing, but they had to march on, without food or adequate clothing, and if they died, they died. The stragglers and the wounded who were too weak to walk were an easy prey to marauding bands of Russians. Those that lived sometimes ate the corpses of their comrades. Many yielded to a craving for sleep and froze to death as they slept.

NAPOLÉON RETURNS TO FRANCE

Napoléon's energy was undiminished. But, in the long days of the retreat, he had too much time for brooding, letting his imagination run on what might be going on at home. News reached him that, in Paris, a republican general called Claude François de Malet had tried to seize power in his absence. He decided to make a dash for home. There was no point in staying with the army, which was already destroyed. Only 4,000 men—out of over 450,000—came back alive. Or, to put it as Napoléon did to the Senate in Paris: "My army has had some losses."

On December 6th, he and de Caulaincourt set out in haste for Paris. On the long, uncomfortable journey, part of it in a covered sleigh, Napoléon chattered endlessly of his future plans, boasting of his love affairs, complaining about the people who had the unenviable task of carrying out his orders. He belittled Wellington's success in Spain, saying "It cannot have any real importance, as I can change the face of affairs when I please." They travelled around the clock, occasionally pausing for a meal or a brief rest. At Posen, in Prussia, Napoléon was delighted to receive affectionate letters from [his wife] Marie-Louise. Finally, on December 18th, they reached their destination, so bedraggled that the porter at the [French royal residence] Tuileries did not recognize them.

CHAPTER 5

NAPOLÉON'S LEGEND AND LEGACY

PEOPLE
WHO MADE
HISTORY

NAPOLÉON BONAPARTE

A Legacy of Political Change

J. Christopher Herold

National Book Award winner J. Christopher Herold
has written extensively about Napoléon, including
The Mind of Napoléon and *Bonaparte in Egypt.* In
the following excerpt from *The Age of Napoléon,*
Herold evaluates how Napoléon influenced the
modern world. Herold contends that the most significant changes the world experienced under
Napoléon were all unintended. He maintains that
Napoléon's conquest of Europe unwittingly spread
the democratic principles of the French Revolution
among the defeated lands. In addition, Herold asserts, Napoléon's oppression and domination of his
new subjects led to the development of feelings of
nationalism and sovereign unity. Herold concludes
that despite Napoléon's best attempts to establish a
new royal dynasty in France and Europe, his efforts
permanently and fatally undermined the institution
of monarchy.

"Greatness has its beauties, but only in retrospect and in the
imagination": thus wrote General [Napoléon] Bonaparte to
General [Victor] Moreau in 1800. His observation helps to
explain why the world, only a few years after sighing with
relief at its delivery from the ogre, began to worship him as
the greatest man of modern times. Napoléon had barely left
the scene when the fifteen years that he had carved out of
world history to create his glory seemed scarcely believable.
Only the scars of the war veterans and the empty places in
the widows' beds seemed to attest to the reality of those
years, and time soon eliminated even these silent witnesses.
What remained, in retrospect and in the imagination, was
legend and symbol. . . .

Excerpted from *The Age of Napoléon,* by J. Christopher Herold. Copyright © 1963 by
American Heritage Publishing Co., Inc. Reprinted by permission of American Heritage
Publishing Co., Inc.

NAPOLÉON IS NOT ENTIRELY RESPONSIBLE

At first glance the balance sheet of Napoléon's adventure seemed to indicate a great deal of waste. After two decades of war, after the loss of far more than a million lives and of millions in property, France emerged reduced to her borders of 1790, saddled with a bill for almost a billion francs in reparations, and with several of her provinces under Allied [England, Austria, Russia, and Prussia] occupation. These, indeed, were the terms imposed on her by the Second Treaty of Paris, signed after Waterloo [in modern Belgium; this battle in 1815 was Napoléon's final military defeat]. Yet in fairness to Napoléon it must be pointed out that the human and material losses should not be debited exclusively to him. The wars that Waterloo concluded had started when he was still a mere lieutenant, and it is more than probable that even if he had died or retired from public life in 1802, there would have been wars all the same. Nor was it he who began the course of conquest that made these wars inevitable; that process began when the French revolutionary government announced that it would liberate the peoples of Europe and gained momentum when its armies occupied Belgium, Holland, the left bank of the Rhine, and northern Italy.

Napoléon's fault was not that he embarked on a career of conquest, but that he was unable or unwilling to stop it while still victorious, or to cut his losses while there was still a chance. His return from [his exile in] Elba was an irresponsible adventure that only a blind admirer would seek to justify; without it France would have escaped foreign occupation, the payment of indemnities, and the humiliation of having to restore, under the terms of the peace treaty, the invaluable art treasures taken from the capitals of Europe. Even so, France was not nearly as exhausted as she seemed: she succeeded in paying the indemnities within the surprisingly short space of three years. By 1818 the last occupation forces evacuated France. . . .

NAPOLÉON: HERO OR DEMIGOD?

Napoléon's impact on the modern imagination has been incalculably great. Who would have dreamed of being a Napoléon before Napoléon? After him, the dream lacked originality. Undoubtedly Hitler, one of the most mediocre figures in world history, dreamed of being Napoléon. One might think that such a disciple would bring his master into disrepute. On the contrary, a comparison between Napoléon and Hitler can only increase one's admiration for Napoléon's sanity, moderation, and economy of cruelty. Napoléon loved only himself, but, unlike Hitler, he hated nobody. In good as in evil, he was without emotion, and he did only so much of either as he believed necessary for his purposes. Moreover, he was the only great dictator of modern times who was not the slave of a particular political doctrine.

As a self-made man and demigod, Napoléon is unique in history and therefore, as it were, timeless. But what of his impact on the modern world—not as a symbol or a mythological figure but as a historical force? How did he find the world, and how did he leave it? Was he, as [Corsican statesman Pasquale] Paoli had predicted, . . . an anachronistic intrusion upon the modern world, or was he a modern, a pathbreaker for a new age? Did his adventure merely interrupt the historic process for two decades, or did it further that process? These are complex questions, and only tentative answers to them are possible.

When he began his career, he found the world in chaos and convulsion. The old order was collapsing; the new order had failed to materialize. Like the hero of some myth or fairy tale, he picked up the pieces of the old order, took advantage of others' quarrels to make himself their master, won kingdoms and vast fortunes, gave wealth and honor to his brothers, sisters, and in-laws, reached for ever more since it was so easy and finally over-reached himself. When his career ended, he left the world still subject to the same explosive tensions that had eased his way to power but so exhausted from his exploits that it postponed its search for a new order by half a century. Perhaps, had he not appeared on the stage, the old order would have been restored fifteen years earlier than it was; on the other hand it is doubtful that the forces that were then shaping today's world—industrial and technological progress, the resulting prosperity of the middle class and the grievances of the laboring class, the general trend toward political equality and national unification— would have been appreciably slower to make themselves felt.

In many ways (though by no means in all), Napoléon was insensitive to the forces that were shaping the future. Except in some scattered remarks he made at St. Helena, when he had time to reflect on the age, he was blind to the potentialities of steam power and of other inventions that were

Napoléon is portrayed as an emperor. Although he created a nobility and disparaged progress, his main achievement was a revolution in techniques of power and of manipulating men.

changing the world. A conservative by temperament, he distrusted innovations of any sort. He sought to establish a dynasty when monarchy was beginning to go out of fashion—and the dynasty he wished to establish was based on the Carolingian model, at that; he created a nobility after a revolution had been fought to abolish it; and in restoring the Church he gave it a position which, as subsequent history has shown, was out of keeping with modern trends.

He disparaged all theories of progress. He paid no attention to the masses—the *canaille*, as he called them—and he willfully ignored the national pride and aspirations of Italians, Germans, Spaniards, Poles, and Russians. He was equally conservative in warfare; his innovations in that art, including his use of unprecedented masses of troops and artillery and his masterly logistics, which made the employment of such masses possible, were important innovations, to be sure, but they grew out of circumstances rather than a wish to revolutionize warfare. In general, he never looked farther ahead than the next day and regarded all experiment as dangerous nonsense. In all these respects—except, perhaps, the military—he cannot be said to have been a modern or to have made a significant contribution to the modern age.

Yet to see in him an anachronistic reincarnation of a hero of antiquity is equally incorrect. His vision of a universal empire may recall [the Roman emperors] Augustus and Diocletian rather than modern times, but who would say that Augustus and Diocletian were not more modern than [French statesman Charles Maurice de] Talleyrand or Metternich [Austrian politician who helped form the victorious alliance against Napoléon]? His passion for uniformity and standardization was decidedly modern. But his main achievement, if it may be called that, was the revolution he brought about in the techniques of power and of manipulating men. His use of the press and of propaganda, his mastery of applied psychology to make people do what he wanted them to do, his rhetoric, his bulletins, his genius at self-dramatization, his flair for pageantry, his superb exploitation of human vanity, ambition, and gullibility, his genius at fanning fear and greed by turns, and, finally, his artful creation of his own legend—all this places him squarely in our own times. Nor has any successful dictator since Napoléon neglected the techniques that he was the first to apply in a systematic way.

Napoléon's Political Legacy

In the science of manipulating men, Napoléon was undoubtedly ahead of his times—a dubious merit. But what was his influence on the historic process of his own times and the decades following? It is generally contended that while he set back the Revolution in France, he promoted the spread of its principles elsewhere, notably in Germany, Italy, and Spain.

This he assuredly did, though not always wittingly or deliberately. The importance of the Civil Code in extending the concept of legal equality has been somewhat exaggerated by Napoléon's apologists. If he helped to sweep away the remnants of feudalism and to arouse the political consciousness of the peoples of Europe, he accomplished this in a negative way. His victories and conquests demonstrated the decrepitude of old institutions and the need for reform; his oppression, his insensitiveness to the national pride of nations other than the French, eventually roused them to action and gave them a sense of dignity and importance that no Holy Alliance could suppress. The Spanish uprising of 1808, the Russian resistance of 1812, the German War of Liberation of 1813 can hardly be said to have been intended by Napoléon; yet they were direct results of his actions, and they changed the world.

Napoléon was not eager to liberate Latin America; yet his aggression in Spain did just that. He was not anxious to make a world power of the United States; yet his sale of the Louisiana Territory did just that. He had no desire to create German unity; yet by reducing the number of sovereignties from more than three hundred to thirty-six (in order to create useful puppet states rather than to benefit Germany) and by fanning German nationalism, which was directed against him, he did more for German unity than any man except Bismarck. There is no evidence that he wished to unite Italy, but he gave the Italians just enough taste of national independence to set the Risorgimento [movement for Italian unification] in motion. He had no desire to strengthen the spiritual power of the pope and sought to foster Gallicanism [devotion to French culture and traditions] instead; the result he achieved was to discredit Gallicanism forever and to give the papacy a moral authority it had not had for centuries. The last thing he desired to do was to undermine the institution of monarchy, on which he based his entire edifice; yet by treating kings as if they were postmasters, by demonstrating the utter moral decay of European monarchy, and by his own anachronistic imperial mummery Napoléon dealt monarchy as destructive a blow as did the executioner who beheaded Louis XVI.

THE TERRIBLE AND THE SUBLIME

One feels at a loss, trying to fit the brief era of Napoléon's domination into the scheme of history. Somehow he does not seem to belong there. His positive achievements merely continued the centralizing trends set by [French cardinal and statesman] Richelieu and Louis XIV [of France]. In nearly all other respects, his historical role was that of an unconscious tool of destruction, clearing the way for a modern age that little resembled the age he thought he was creating. The first of the modern dictators, he was less the creature of his times than were his successors and imitators, and he remains unique. Some have found it convenient, therefore, to discount the entire Napoléonic era as an adventure, brilliant but hopeless, made possible by the chaos of the times, paid for by millions of lives, unnecessary and senseless—a pageant of classical glory interrupting the prosaic evolution of modern industrial society. What the historical temperament discounts as a freakish intrusion, the poetic temperament extols as a creation of the will and a manifestation of energy, complete in itself, like a work of art, in which the terrible is transmuted into the sublime, and which has no other purpose than itself.

And yet, unnecessary as the adventure may have been except for the glorification of one man, it is impossible to enter that man's tomb without experiencing a poignant emotion. His fatal attraction remains alive, even to those who would defend themselves against it. The conquered flags, worn thin as cobwebs, mere ghosts of flags, conjure up the ghosts of glory. "What a romance my life has been!" Napoléon exclaimed once. What an epic he gave mankind to remember! Who else could give the world such a spectacle? What poet could imagine what he did in action? What an artist! What deception!

Napoléon and Hitler

Desmond Seward

Historians have found several parallels between Nazi dictator Adolf Hitler and Napoléon Bonaparte. In the following excerpt from *Napoléon and Hitler*, author Desmond Seward notes that not only are there similarities in their backgrounds, but also in their single-minded determination to rule as much of the world as they could conquer. Both were gamblers, he maintains, who wagered the fate of their countries to satisfy their personal ambitions. Seward points out that Napoléon's success might well have inspired Hitler's need for power and conquest. But he also acknowledges that their differences are just as pronounced; while Hitler leaves almost no legacy except shame and fear, Napoléon created modern France.

> I certainly deprecate any comparison between Herr Hitler and Napoléon: I do not wish to insult the dead.
>
> *Winston Churchill*, speech at Harrow in December 1940

Others besides Winston Churchill may think it blasphemy to compare Napoléon and [German dictator Adolf] Hitler. Certainly there are many differences—not least the relative duration of their careers. The Emperor was forty-four when he fell from power, the age of the Führer when he achieved it. Yet undeniably there are resemblances too; their rise from obscurity, their military domination over Europe, their tyranny and contempt for human life, their megalomania and inability to compromise, their hubris. No one can ever be really sure that a nuclear war or an economic collapse will not occur, creating just the sort of chaos from which their like might emerge again. An examination of the two men's careers and a pinpointing of the qualities they share may provide a means of identifying future 'saviours,' as well as casting fresh light on both, and especially upon Hitler.

In 1941 Professor Pieter Geyl of the University of Utrecht

Excerpted from *Napoléon and Hitler: A Comparative Biography*, by Desmond Seward (London: Harrap, 1988). Copyright © Desmond Seward 1988. Reprinted by permission of the author.

was by some miracle released from Buchenwald, returning to internment in occupied Holland. He spent the rest of the war working on his great study of Napoléon's historians, *Napoléon: For and Against.* In this he says that one cannot avoid comparing the Emperor and the Führer, since the resemblances are 'too striking'; that he had 'hated the dictator in Napoléon long before the evil presence of Hitler began darkening our lives,' but has 'nowhere worked it out.' He also admits that 'one almost feels as if one should ask pardon of the Emperor for mentioning his name in one breath with that of the other.'. . .

HITLER AND NAPOLÉON COMPARED

No one will dispute that Hitler was more evil than the Emperor, did evil on a far greater scale. A liberal like Lord [John Emerich] Acton could call Napoléon 'the most splendid genius that has appeared on earth', and he still inspires some very unlikely people. No one denies that he created modern France, while nothing remains of the Führer's Germany save the autobahns. [British historian] Hugh Trevor-Roper likens the latter's mind to 'some barbarian monolith, the expression of giant strength and savage genius, surrounded by a festering heap of refuse.'

Even so, the resemblances are inescapable. Each was a foreigner in an adopted country, self-made—the Emperor an uprooted squireen [a gentleman in a small way], the Führer a rootless *petit-bourgeois* [lower middle class]. They appeared from nowhere to become 'saviours' of their new countries; Napoléon was not a Frenchman but a Corsican who kept an Italian accent till he was nearly thirty, while Hitler never lost his Austrian accent. Each was a loner despising the rest of humanity. The Emperor believed that any man—or woman—could be bought, while Hitler declared 'I have come not to make men better but to make them worse.' (Mme de Staël described the 'hall-mark of Bonaparte's rule' as 'profound contempt for the riches of human nature.') Napoléon and Hitler loathed intellectuals, suppressing freedom of thought by means of censorship and secret police. Emperor and Führer restored briefly their countries' prosperity and self-confidence, and then conquered most of Europe through ruthless diplomacy and war. Both destroyed themselves by invading Russia. Hitler echoed Napoléon's fear (voiced on St Helena) that 'the Cossacks will rule Europe', and was very conscious of his predecessor's failure—after his armies had survived the winter of 1941 he boasted: 'We mastered a destiny which broke another man 130 years ago.'

Admittedly Hitler's hero, in so far as he ever had one, was Frederick the Great [of Prussia], as creator of the *Preussensgeist* [Prussian spirit]—that terrifyingly dynamic compound of militarism and State service, of discipline and precision. In the Führer's eyes Napoléon never achieved anything like such distinction. Yet while he sometimes looked to the old King for inspiration he must have been keenly aware how many of his problems had been those of the man whom he described . . . as 'that unique military genius, the Corsican Napoléon.'

The Emperor and the Führer were gamblers who kept the game playing until the very end, whatever the cost to their peoples. 'Conquest has made me what I am, conquest alone can maintain me,' Napoléon [said]. 'Small change' was what he called the French dead at Eylau [in Russia]. Both conscripted relative children into their armies, Napoléon the 'Marie Louises' (fifteen-year-olds) in 1814, Hitler the Hitler Youth in 1945. The Emperor bragged 'A man like me cares little about losing the lives of a million men,' the Führer 'I can send the flower of German youth into the hell of war without the slightest pity.' Napoléon's threat 'I shall bury the world beneath my ruin' was repeated by Hitler—'We may be destroyed but, if we are, we'll drag the world down with us, a world in flames.' The former anticipated the Führer in preparing a *Götterdämmerung*-like fight [a final battle] to the death in his capital. In 1814 he ordered that Paris must never be evacuated even if this meant its destruction. . . .

But one must agree with Geyl that the Emperor can only benefit from comparison with the Führer—the worst of his crimes cannot possibly match Adolf Hitler's murder of the Jewish people.

Napoléon, Hitler, and Clausewitz

There is a subtle link between the pair, which emerges only when they are compared. It is contained in the writings of that baneful genius Carl von Clausewitz, one of the brilliant group of soldiers who rebuilt the Prussian army after its humiliating defeat by Napoléon in 1806. Something of an outsider on account of bourgeois origins and spurious nobility (his father had merely assumed the 'von'), he was never entirely at ease in the exclusively noble Prussian officer corps, although he joined it at the age of twelve, while his interest in new ideas incurred suspicions of 'Jacobinism.' His primary concern was to produce a military science capable of meeting and overcoming the 'nation in arms' concept developed by the French; he foresaw further great wars, and was determined that Prussia should emerge triumphant from them. He remained essentially a Prussian expansionist, his views on Poland anticipating in some ways those of Hitler. It has been claimed that his influence in Germany was among the causes of both world wars. As a 'military philosopher' he tried to see both sides of every question, and since he had a mind shaped (at second hand) by [philosopher Immanuel] Kant, his meaning is often over-subtle or ambiguous—he himself wrote that his work was 'open to endless misconceptions.' The Führer was to be the ultimate misinterpreter of Clausewitz.

A comparison of the Emperor and Hitler reveals the enormous influence on the latter of Clausewitz's view of Napoléon. Most of the Führer's biographers refer to his being a disciple of the Prussian general, yet not one has sufficiently examined this aspect, let alone Hitler's indirect debt to the Emperor through the latter's writings. Clausewitz had had first-hand experience of Napoléonic methods—from the other side. . . . He venerated Napoléon as a genius, for breaking 'the rules of civilised warfare.' Even if he never totally understood the Emperor's strategic method, he none the less grasped the basic ideas behind it, and has been described as 'distilling Napoléon into theory.'

VOM KRIEGE AND *MEIN KAMPF*

There is no doubt that the Führer studied Clausewitz—even if that passionate Clausewitzian, the late Raymond Aron, could not bear to believe it. *Vom Kriege* ('On War'), Clausewitz's masterpiece, was almost certainly among the 'books on war' which he is reported to have read before 1914. In *Mein Kampf* [*My Struggle*] he quotes it with savage approval, and in a speech at Munich in 1934 accused his audience of never having read Clausewitz, or if they had, of not knowing how to apply him to modern circumstances. On at least one occasion he reminded his generals that he knew Clausewitz, while Keitel stated at Nuremburg, that during the war Hitler had spent whole nights studying him. Admittedly, as Aron emphasizes, there have been many enthusiastic readers of Clausewitz, but few careful ones. It is unlikely that the Führer ever understood properly the theories of this most complex of military philosophers, which may be why historians have underestimated his influence on Hitler. Yet the Führer acknowledged Clausewitz alone as his intellectual master. It is only reasonable to suppose that he was fascinated by the many desperate situations so closely paralleling his own which are described and analysed in *Vom Kriege*— the 1812 campaign, and Napoléon's last-ditch defensive battles in 1814 being the most obvious. As a man who habitually read into a situation what he wished to believe, he may very well have extracted from the book merely what he wanted. Even so, a careful study of *Vom Kriege* casts considerable light on Hitler's mind and on why he reached a number of historic decisions.

ENIGMAS

It is the enigma presented by the Führer that makes him unique, not only the vast scale of his wickedness. . . . Yet we know far more about him than about earlier tyrants. The enigma consists in his possessing so many undeniable gifts and likeable qualities, besides those which can be immediately recognized as evil. It is this extraordinary mixture which gives the man and his career their ultimate horror. Only by appreciating Hitler's good points can one appreciate the full extent of his savagery and depravity.

Napoléon is almost as baffling for much the same reason, and he was given time to fabricate his own legend on St Helena, shaping his own image in history. (For all that, none of the many thousand books about him agree.) Luckily, the Führer was not given the opportunity similarly to sift the facts in his own favour. However, if the Emperor possessed a surprisingly similar combination of good and evil qualities, he is less of an enigma.

THE EUROPEAN DIMENSION

There is an aspect of the two men which tends to be overlooked, their European dimension. The years from the Napoléonic wars to Hitler's mark the height of the European hegemony over the rest of the world, a hegemony that has now vanished, perhaps for ever. Admittedly, the Emperor began the irreversible destruction of the old hierarchical, Christian Europe and the Führer completed it. Even so, the legend which Napoléon afterwards disseminated from his exile on St Helena included a vision of a united Europe of the future. It can be argued that to some extent he prepared the way for unification; his creation of a single West German state (the Confederation of the Rhine) and of a single North Italian state (the Kingdom of Italy) undoubtedly contributed. And though Hitler ruined Europe, destroying its dominance, he did at least demolish some of the obstacles which stood in the way of a united continent. Napoléon called the continent 'a rotten old whore whom I shall treat as I please,' while in 1943 [Nazi leader Joseph] Goebbels recorded the Führer's 'unshakeable conviction that the Reich will be master of all Europe'—two years later, just before his death, Hitler said of the continent, 'I had to rape it in order to possess it.'

No doubt, as Geyl emphasizes, 'under Napoléon, French civilisation (albeit stifled and narrowed by him) still accompanied the conquest, while the character of the conquest that it has been the lot of our generation to undergo is not compatible with any civilisation at all.' The French brought their social and legal revolution with them, so that everyone became equal before the law in much of western Europe. Even so, they imposed these benefits as conquerors. Hippolyte Taine, perhaps the most formidable intellect among all the critics of [Napoléon], shudders at what might have happened had he triumphed over the Russians in 1812:

> At best a European empire secretly undermined by a European resistance, an external France imposed by force on an enslaved continent, with French commissioners and military governors at St. Petersburg and Riga as at Danzig, Hamburg, Amsterdam, Lisbon, Barcelona and Trieste, every available Frenchman employed from Cadiz to Moscow in maintaining and administering the conquest; every available young man conscripted each year and, should he escape, reconscripted by decree, the entire male population employed in oppression; no other prospect for an educated or an uneducated man, no other career military or civil, but extended duty as soldier, excise officer or policeman in the role of spy or bully, employed to hold down the subjected and extort taxes; to confiscate and burn merchandise, to catch smugglers and crush the obstinate.

Taine wrote in the 1880s, never dreaming that a very similar German hegemony would be established sixty years later, which would offer as its highest careers those of spy and bully.

Essentially each man was an opportunist on a colossal scale. 'His ideas about the history of the Revolution were astonishingly superficial and defective,' the former deputy Jean Charles Bailleul wrote of Napoléon. 'He used just so much of it as he needed to construct a régime which was neither old nor new. This misunderstanding, whether deliberate or unintentional, of men and principles had a most disastrous effect on his career.' Hermann Rauschning—also a contemporary observer—said of Hitler in 1939: 'He damped down the Socialist tendencies in the movement and brought the Nationalist ones into the foreground. He was out to gain powerful patrons and friends who could help the movement into power.' Rauschning discerned that his movement had 'no fixed aims, either economic or political, either in home or foreign affairs.' Both in Napoléonic France and in Hitlerian Germany, there was only one leader. Everything, whether human beings or principles, was subject to his devouring, insatiable egotism. . . .

In 1811 Napoléon asked an aghast [French Minister of Police Joseph] Fouché: 'How can I help it when all this power is sweeping me on to world dictatorship?' After conquering Russia he intended to assemble an army at Tiflis, and then send it through Afghanistan into India. In 1942 Hitler told [Nazi leader] Albert Speer that after Russia's defeat 'a mere 20 or 30 divisions' would be all that was necessary to conquer India. As young men the Emperor and the Führer had little in common—a Corsican soldier and a failed Austrian 'artist.' What united them at their zenith was the demonic process of corruption by power.

Lessons from Napoléon's Career

Alistair Horne

Alistair Horne, who was awarded the French Legion of Honor for his work as a historian, reviews Napoléon's career to determine what lessons can be learned. According to Horne, a primary lesson is that military conquest only leads to more conquest in order to keep possession of the lands already conquered. He argues that such a policy inevitably leads to the victorious country spreading its resources too thin and is therefore vulnerable to attacks from its enemies. But perhaps the most important lesson from Napoléon's defeat, Horne contends, is the value of coalitions in defeating a common enemy. Horne is the author of *How Far from Austerlitz? Napoléon 1805–1815*, from which this essay is excerpted.

The advent [of the reign] of Louis Napoléon [Napoléon's nephew, who ruled France 1852–1870] brought with it a huge rekindling of interest in the First Empire in France. Books on Napoléon became a new growth industry. But were the lessons learnt? What were they? Following Napoléon's hour of greatest triumph at Tilsit, in 1807, France did undoubtedly experience a period of unprecedented economic prosperity. But it was illusory; as with [Nazi dictator Adolf] Hitler's Reich [period of rule] in the halcyon years of 1940–2, it was largely at the cost of subjugated neighbours. As such, inevitably, it built up a massive reservoir of resentment against Napoléon, which in due course would play its role in his downfall. Also, the Continental System [Napoléon's economic blockade of England] never really worked; as late as 1810, embattled Britain would still somehow be receiving over 80 per cent of her wheat imports from France or her allies, while in the long run its failure would turn out to be fatal for France herself.

SIMILARITIES WITH THE WORLD WARS

British experience of the Napoléonic blockade was, a century later, to have a most important influence in the shaping of grand strategy in both world wars. Indeed, in the Second World War the timetable for Britain shows a curious similarity to what happened during the Napoléonic Wars:

- defeat of the First Coalition (1939–40)
- banishment of Britain from Europe (Dunkirk)
- failure of invasion from Europe and triumph of sea power (1940–1)
- formation of new coalitions but continuing enemy land triumphs (1941–2)
- backbone of enemy broken in Russia (1942–4)

Of course, the parallel ends there. In 1815, with Napoléon defeated and the rest of Europe exhausted by war and blockade, the field was left clear for Britain 'to become the workshop and the banker of the world, the very thing Napoléon had sought to prevent'; but in 1945 it was Britain that emerged devitalized.

Once the spirit of Tilsit [Treaties of Tilsit followed Napoléon's military victories of Prussians and Russians, extending France's rule to include most of Europe] had begun to wear thin, more than any other factor it was the Continental System and its consequences that led Napoléon on the road to Moscow in 1812; just as it was, still, the English dynamo and her treasury that would continue to sustain his enemies. ('Russia was the last resource of England,' Napoléon admitted on St Helena. 'The peace of the world rested with Russia. Alas! English gold proved more powerful than my plans.')

MILITARY LESSONS

For the *Grande Armée* [Napoléon's army], Tilsit was a kind of watershed, after which it never seemed quite so good again. First of all, with longed for peace at hand it was hard to keep up the old revolutionary fervour, let alone the standard of training with which it had marched out of the Camp of Boulogne in 1805. While recruitment grew increasingly inefficient, losses had left their mark, particularly those suffered at Eylau [Napoléon's first major military stalemate], and particularly among the *cadres* [a basic military unit]. Then came the 'Spanish Ulcer' [Spain's refusal to accept French rule resulting in war between France and Spain, 1808–1814]. . . . Some of the marshals began to wax fat on the fruits (and loots) of peace. They took to quarrelling with each other and disobeying orders. As a result of all this, after 1807 units of the *Grande Armée* were less capable of performing the complex manoeuvres that had brought victory at Austerlitz [considered Napoléon's greatest military victory in 1805] and Auerstädt [Napoléon's 1806 victory over Prussia], and they indulged more in costly mass tactics—such as were to prove Napoléon's undoing at Waterloo [in 1815, Napoléon's final defeat].

Other enemy armies began at last to study and emulate the Napoléonic technique. Soon after 1807 it was discovered that Napoléon's valuable shock weapon, his shield of skirmishers, could no longer shake a prepared enemy line. The Emperor also found himself fighting in countries where, for the first time, the inhabitants would prove virulently hostile. Then, with each succeeding battle, the forces present grew steadily larger. This had a disastrous effect on Napoléon's highly personal style of command. The scale of operations in Russia (as Hitler in his turn was to discover) was simply too great for one man to control. As the armies grew larger, so did the casualty lists, until, at grim Leipzig in 1813, a terrible battle of attrition cost Napoléon five times his losses at Austerlitz. The *Grande Armée* never recovered.

The lessons to be derived from Napoléon's amazing run of victories in 1805–7 are those that have been learnt (or not learnt) by military adventurers through the ages, from Xerxes [of Persia, sixth century B.C. ruler] to Hitler—there is seldom such a thing as a *limited* victory. One conquest only leads on, ineluctably, to another, to protect what has already been won. Napoléon's wars on the continent gained him no real friends, . . . only crushed enemies: 'Prussia vanquished but fuming, Austria secretly implacable', in the words of [twentieth century French president Adolphe] Thiers. Resurgent already in 1809, only to be knocked down again at Wagram [Napoléon's 1809 victory over Austria], Austria nevertheless would be inexorably at Napoléon's throat once more in the Leipzig campaign of 1813. As far as the Russian colossus was concerned, although Napoléon had left Tilsit persuaded that he had effectively seduced the Tsar, it was clearly a seduction requiring constant attention and refurbishment. For it was upon Russia's continuing benevolence that Napoléon's grandiose future schemes had depended. Unlike Austria and Prussia, she alone had not been invaded and subjugated on her own territory; her armies had been defeated in a series of great battles, but all of them on somebody else's soil, and in terms of manpower she still remained the world's most powerful land force. Though Russia was defeated in 1805 and 1807, invaded and desperately mauled in 1812, in 1814 it was the Tsar's armies that would be in Paris, forcing Napoléon to abdicate.

BRITAIN'S DETERMINATION

Yet, all the time, it was Britain's gold and her inflexible will to bring Napoléon down which helped breathe life into coalition after coalition. The cost to Britain had been enormous: over the whole twenty years of war, she had paid out in subsidies to her allies nearly £66 million, and almost half of this, disproportionately, in the last three years; between 1793 and 1815 government spending had risen from 6 per cent of the national income to 25 per cent and the national debt had soared from £245m to £834m—equal to £43 per head of every man, woman and child. Figures for overall deaths caused by the twenty years of war are uncertain, though one historian, Rory Muir, puts them at between 200,000 and 250,000 (probably most from disease); a total which, from Britain's far smaller population, he equates (strikingly) with the scale of losses (though much more compressed in terms of time) suffered in 1914–18. But what this expenditure bought for Britain, a 'Pax Britannica' enduring over the next century, derived almost entirely from the fact (and a fact that is often overlooked) that although (as in 1939–45) without Russia there could have been no Allied triumph, at Waterloo, the final round of the Napoléonic Wars was won by a *British*—and not a Russian, Austrian, or even Prussian victory. The settlement of 1815 inevitably invites comparisons with that of 1945; but the difference is that the defeat of Nazi Germany left no acceptable regime with which to negotiate, no tame Bourbons waiting in the wings to be restored—and no [French statesman] Talleyrand to negotiate on behalf of the defeated. Yet the statesmen of 1815 surely deserve History's recognition for the moderate and enduring peace which they constructed.

Britain's determination to defeat Napoléon was finally realized in the battle of Waterloo, which marked a change in the direction of the world.

As Victor Hugo remarked, Waterloo was not just a battle: it marked a change in the direction of the world. One of the most formidable changes of that direction lay in the future of Prussia, so deeply humiliated in the Jena Campaign of 1806. . . . Despite Talleyrand's warning, Napoléon had committed his gravest error at Tilsit by imposing the harsh terms which, *inter alia*, deprived Prussia of half her territories and subjected the remainder to a degrading occupation. At Jena he had destroyed a feudal army, as well as the feudal nation to which it belonged. But he would be responsible for the *national* army which, out of the ashes, would arise to smash him at Leipzig, in the War of the Nations of 1813—and ultimately destroy him at Waterloo. Although Napoléon had defeated every professional army in Europe, it was the sheer numerical weight of the resurgent peoples that finally ground him down. As he himself once confessed, 'Against greatly superior forces, it is possible to win a battle, but hardly a war.' In the long run (as Hitler was to discover), military brilliance is not enough; numbers are what count.

Beyond the context of the Napoléonic Wars, in the longer term Prussia's humiliation at Jena was perhaps to produce

the most dire political consequences for successive generations of Napoléon's adopted countrymen, and indeed for all
Europe. His attempts to sweep away the medieval structure
of the German states and 're-order' it—much as he had
done in north Italy—would unwittingly pave the way for
German unification. Out of it would emerge a new super-
state east of the Rhine: the Prussian-led German Reich.
Sixty-five years after Austerlitz, it would inflict upon
Napoléon's own nephew as shattering a defeat as any he
had ever dealt out. The technique of conscription introduced by Napoléon to create his mass armies was to mark
the beginning of the era of total war—'a backward step for
mankind', remarks André Maurois in his *History of France.*
Three times in the century that lay ahead, such a mass
army would . . . lay waste to France.

One of the great ironies of Napoléon's years of triumph lies
in what he did to the ethos of the French Revolution, the im-
petus of which had so materially aided him in his conquests.
While at home, in France, he had put into reverse many of its
principles, he carried those same principles in the baggage-
train of the *Grande Armée* to the nations it conquered. Born
and bred in Paris, ideals of liberty, egalitarianism and nationalism had been unleashed among all the European peoples, and—long after Napoléon's conquests were forgotten—
these would clash resoundingly with the Old Order. . . .

British 'Eurosceptics' of the 1990s might be forgiven, if
in their gloomier moments, they were to foresee that by the
two hundredth anniversary of Waterloo, in 2015, most of
Napoléon's social agenda for Europe will have been achieved
(though, more probably, the principal beneficiaries will by
then prove to be the heirs to Kaiser Wilhelm [of Germany]).
Yet, if the prolonged struggle over Napoléonic hegemony has
any lesson, or moral, useful to Britain today, it is perhaps the
value of coalitions. Muddled and inefficient as they may be,
two world wars and a cold war show that, in the long run,
they win wars—and possibly prevent them. Powers, however
strong, that exist alone, isolated, are usually doomed.

Discussion Questions

Chapter One

1. Frank McLynn describes the adult Napoléon as having been deeply influenced by the violent history of his Corsican homeland as well as by his "ill-matched parents." What specific traits, values, and beliefs did Napoléon receive from each?

2. According to George Gordon Andrews, what social policies and military innovations did Napoléon inherit from the French Revolution? Do you think the French were better off because of these changes? Why or why not?

Chapter Two

1. Napoléon's Civil Code is credited with changing not only the laws of France, but also most of Europe. What specific legal innovations does author Martyn Lyons credit to Napoléon's Civil Code? Which laws do you agree or disagree with? Why?

2. Will Durant and Ariel Durant describe Napoléon's radical reform of France's educational system. What was Napoléon's motivation for this drastic renovation?

3. The Concordat between Pope Pius VII and Napoléon was designed to normalize relationships between France and the Catholic Church. According to Geoffrey Ellis, what specific concessions did Napoléon agree to? Do you think Napoléon was right to make this agreement, even though it contradicted the tenets of the French Revolution?

4. Michael Polowetzky's article shows Napoléon to have been deeply interested in France's theater productions. What did Napoléon hope to gain from monitoring and interfering with the theater? Should a government have the right to censor works of art, even if it believes it is for the ultimate benefit of the people?

5. By 1810, Napoléon had alienated much of the population throughout the French Empire. To what does author Roger

Dufraisse attribute this widespread disillusionment? In what specific ways did the people show their contempt?

CHAPTER THREE

1. The Continental System was designed to destroy the economy of England. In what ways was it successful and in what ways was it unsuccessful? Why did Napoléon choose this option over a military invasion? What was the result of the Continental System on France's allies?

2. Ruling conquered lands proved to be a great challenge for Napoléon. According to Michael Broers, what were the obstacles he had to overcome? Even in places where Napoléon's rule brought social modernization and economic improvement, do you think the population was justified in rebelling?

CHAPTER FOUR

1. What military strategies does Robert B. Holtman attribute to Napoléon that made him one of the most successful—and studied—generals of all time? What military theories did he inherit from the French Revolution and how did he change them to make them more effective?

2. At the Tuileries Palace, Napoléon slaughtered many Parisians. Why does Owen Connelly believe this demonstration of ruthlessness advanced Napoléon's career? Do you think Napoléon was justified in the severity of his actions?

3. According to Jean Tulard, what did Napoléon hope to gain for himself and for France by his campaign against Egypt? What actual gains were achieved? Is the invasion of another country justified if it brings about enormous advancements in knowledge of science and history?

4. Anthony Masters describes a disastrous French campaign against Russia. What compelled Napoléon to embark on this campaign? What was the Russian military strategy against France? What were the contributing nonmilitary causes to Napoléon's defeat?

CHAPTER FIVE

1. J. Christopher Herold suggests that many of the changes Napoléon brought about were unintended. What were those changes? How did they come about?

2. Napoléon and Hitler are often compared. Why? Author Desmond Seward outlines what he considers the similarities and differences. What are they? To what other past

and present world leaders might you compare Napoléon? Explain why.

3. What are the major lessons Alistair Horne believes can be learned from Napoléon's career? Do you think twentieth-century history shows that we have learned those lessons? Give examples.

APPENDIX OF DOCUMENTS

DOCUMENT 1: NAPOLÉON DEFENDS HIS RULE

On May 1, 1816, while in exile on St. Helena, Napoléon defended his actions as a ruler to his companion, Emmanuel Las Cases. He claims that many of his actions, which historians may fault him for, were done out of necessity, not personal glory. Even his own ambition, he argues, was of the "noblest kind."

"I closed the gulf of anarchy and cleared [away] the chaos. I purified the Revolution, dignified Nations and established Kings. I excited every kind of emulation, rewarded every kind of merit, and extended the limits of glory! This is at least something! And on what point can I be assailed on which an historian could not defend me? Can it be for my intentions? But even here I can find absolution. Can it be for my despotism? It may be demonstrated that the Dictatorship was absolutely necessary. Will it be said that I restrained liberty? It can be proved that licentiousness, anarchy, and the greatest irregularities still haunted the threshold of freedom. Shall I be accused of having been too fond of war? It can be shown that I always received the first attack. Will it be said that I aimed at universal monarchy? It can be proved that this was merely the result of fortuitous circumstances, and that our enemies themselves led me step by step to this determination. Lastly, shall I be blamed for my ambition? This passion I must doubtless be allowed to have possessed, and that in no small degree; but, at the same time, my ambition was of the highest and noblest kind that ever, perhaps, existed! . . . That of establishing and of consecrating the Empire of reason, and the full exercise and complete enjoyment of all the human faculties! And here the historian will probably feel compelled to regret that such ambition should not have been fulfilled and gratified!". . . Then after a few moments of silent reflection, "This," said the Emperor, "is my whole history in a few words."

David L. Dowd, *Source Problems in World Civilizations: Napoléon, Was He the Heir of the Revolution?* Chicago: Holt, Rinehart and Winston, 1957, pp. 17–18.

DOCUMENT 2: THE EVILS OF REVOLUTION

On another occasion during his St. Helena exile, Napoléon dictated his thoughts on September 3, 1816, to his companion, Emmanuel

Las Cases. Ironically, though Napoléon personally benefited enormously from the French Revolution, he argues here that revolution makes the participants' lives miserable and that only future generations enjoy its benefits.

"No social revolution ever takes place unaccompanied by violence. ... The reign of terror commenced on the 4th of August [1789], with the abolition of titles of nobility, tithes, and feudal rights, the wrecks of which were scattered among the multitude, who then, for the first time, understood and felt really interested in the Revolution. Before this period there was so much of dependence and religious spirit among the people, that many doubted whether the harvest could be gathered in without the King and the tithes.

"A revolution," concluded the Emperor, "is one of the greatest evils by which mankind can be visited. It is the scourge of the generation by whom it is brought about; and all the advantages it procures cannot make amends for the misery with which it embitters the lives of those who participate in it." ... "The best-founded revolutions, at the outset, bring universal destruction in their train; the advantages they may produce are reserved for a future age. Ours seems to have been an irresistible fatality: It was a moral eruption, which could no more be prevented than a physical eruption. When the chemical combinations necessary to produce the latter are complete, it bursts forth: in France the moral combinations which produce a revolution had arrived at maturity, and the explosion accordingly took place."

David L. Dowd, *Source Problems in World Civilizations: Napoléon, Was He the Heir of the Revolution?* Chicago: Holt, Rinehart and Winston, 1957, pp. 7–8.

DOCUMENT 3: THE CIVIL CODE AND MARRIAGE

On March 21, 1804, a new Civil Code was adopted that largely did away with the feudal system of privilege for the aristocracy. The Code, renamed the Code Napoléon in 1807, was adopted by thirty-five countries and adapted in some form by thirty-five others. Although the Code did bring about uniform civil equality and opportunity for most French people, some groups—such as women, laborers, and black slaves—were excluded from enjoying these expanded rights. The following selection from the Civil Code demonstrates this inequality toward women.

Chapter VI. Of the Respective Rights and Duties of Husband and Wife

213. A husband owes protection to his wife; a wife obedience to her husband.

214. A wife is bound to live with her husband and to follow him wherever he deems proper to reside.

215. A wife cannot sue in court without the consent of her husband, even if she is a public tradeswoman or if there is no community or she is separated as to property. . . .

217. A wife, even when there is no community, or when she is separated as to property, cannot give, convey, mortgage, or acquire property, with or without consideration, without the husband joining in the instrument or giving his written consent. . . .

229. A husband may sue for a divorce on account of the wife's adultery.

230. A wife may sue for divorce only in the case in which the husband introduces a permanent mistress into the marital household. . . .

308. A wife against whom a separation from bed and board has been decreed on account of adultery shall be sentenced . . . to imprisonment . . . for a period of not less than three months and not more than two years. . . .

340. The attempt to prove paternity is forbidden. . . .

341. Proof of maternal descent is allowed. . . .

776. Married women cannot lawfully accept a succession without the consent of their husbands. . . .

905. A married woman cannot make a gift or donation during her lifetime without . . . the consent of her husband. . . .

934. A married woman cannot accept a gift or donation without her husband's consent. . . .

David L. Dowd, *Source Problems in World Civilizations: Napoléon, Was He the Heir of the Revolution?* Chicago: Holt, Rinehart and Winston, 1957, p. 43.

DOCUMENT 4: THE CONCORDAT

Napoléon reversed the French Revolution's anti–Catholic Church policy by negotiating an agreement, the Concordat of 1801, with the church. Though this agreement recognized Catholicism as the religion of the majority of French people, it still maintained strict governmental controls over the church's political and social influence. The following excerpt from the Concordat shows the delicate balance between religious freedom and governmental authority.

The Concordat, 26 Messidor, Year IX–18 Germinal, Year X (July 15, 1801–April 8, 1802)

Convention between the French Government and His Holiness Pius VII

The Government of the French Republic recognizes that the Roman, Catholic, and Apostolic religion is the religion of the great majority of French citizens.

His Holiness likewise recognizes that this same religion has derived and at this moment again expects the greatest benefit and grandeur from the establishment of Catholic worship in France and from the personal profession of it made by the Consuls of the Republic.

Consequently, after this mutual recognition, as well for the benefit of religion and the maintenance of internal tranquillity, they have agreed as follows:

1. The Catholic, Apostolic, and Roman religion shall be freely exercised in France: its worship shall be public, and in conformity with the police regulations which the Government shall deem necessary for the public tranquillity.

2. A new circumscription of the French dioceses shall be made by the Holy See in cooperation with the Government.

3. His Holiness shall declare to the titular French bishops that he with firm confidence expects from them, for the benefit of peace and unity, every sort of sacrifice, even that of their sees. . . .

4. The First Consul of the Republic shall make appointments . . . to the archbishoprics and bishoprics of the new circumscription. His Holiness shall confer the canonical institution, following the forms established in relation to France before the change of government.

5. The nominations to the bishoprics which shall be vacant in the future shall likewise be made by the First Consul, and the canonical institution shall be given by the Holy See. . . .

6. Before entering upon their functions, the bishops shall take directly, at the hands of the First Consul, the following oath of fidelity:

"I swear and promise to God, upon the Holy Scriptures, to remain in obedience and fidelity to the government established by the constitution of the French Republic. I also promise not to have any intercourse, nor to assist by any counsel, nor to support any league, either within or without, which is inimical to the public tranquillity; and if, within my diocese or elsewhere, I learn that anything to the prejudice of the state is being contrived, I will make it known to the Government."

8. The following prayer shall be repeated at the end of divine service in all the Catholic churches of France:

God save the Republic, God save the Consuls.

David L. Dowd, *Source Problems in World Civilizations: Napoléon, Was He the Heir of the Revolution?* Chicago: Holt, Rinehart and Winston, 1957, pp. 29–30.

DOCUMENT 5: THE POLITICAL USE OF RELIGION

In the following dictation given in 1816, Napoléon explains his motivations in going against the spirit of the French Revolution by restoring some of the Catholic Church's influence in France. Although Napoléon states that he could have favored Protestantism just as easily as Catholicism, he chose the latter to prevent religious wars from breaking out among the French. He hoped that by bringing Catholicism back into favor he would achieve some influence over Pope Pius VII.

When I seized the helm, I already had settled ideas about all the principal elements that make for the cohesion of society. I had fully weighed the importance of religion. My mind was made up, and I resolved to restore the Church. But it is hard to believe how much resistance I had to overcome in order to bring Catholicism back. I would have found more willing support if I had hoisted the Protestant banner. . . . There is no doubt that after the disorder to which I succeeded, in the ruins on which I found myself placed, I was free to choose between Catholicism and Protestantism. It is also true to say that the times entirely favored the latter. But, quite aside from the fact that my native religion really meant something to me, my decision was founded on reasons of the highest order. If I had proclaimed Protestantism, what would have been the result? I would have divided France into two parties of approximately equal strength, whereas I wanted to have no more parties at all. I would have revived the fury of religious quarrels just when the spirit of the times and my own will aimed at making them vanish forever. In rending each other, these two parties would have annihilated France and made her the slave of Europe—when I had the ambition to make her Europe's mistress. With Catholicism, I was sure to succeed in all my great plans. At home, in France, the majority was sure to swallow up the minority, and I was resolved to treat the minority on a basis of equality such that soon there would have been no noticeable difference. Abroad, Catholicism was to keep the pope favorably disposed toward me—and what with my influence and my troops in Italy, I had reason to hope that sooner or later, one way or another, I would end up by controlling that pope. And after that—what influence! What a lever on public opinion throughout the world!

J. Christopher Herold, ed., *The Mind of Napoléon: A Selection from His Written and Spoken Words*, trans. J. Christopher Herold. New York: Columbia University Press, 1955, pp. 105–106.

DOCUMENT 6: THE ORGANIC ARTICLES

Faced with strong anti-Catholic opposition to his Concordat in both the government and the military, Napoléon added a list of even stricter regulations on the Catholic Church. These regulations, passed in 1802, were known as the Organic Articles, and were seen for the first time by Pope Pius VII after they were published in French newspapers.

The Organic Articles for the Catholic Church, 18 Germinal, Year X (April 8, 1802)

   Title I. Of the Regime of the Catholic Church in Its Relations with the Rights and the Policy of the State

   1. No bull, brief, . . . or other document from the court of Rome may be put into effect, without the authorization of the Government.

   2. No person calling himself nuncio, legate, . . . or any other denomination, without the same authorization, can exercise any function relative to the affairs of the Gallican church.

   3. Decrees of foreign synods, even those of general councils, cannot be published in France before the Government has [approved them].

4. No national or metropolitan council, no diocesan synod, no deliberative assembly, shall take place without the express permission of the Government.

5. All the ecclesiastical offices shall be free except for offerings authorized and fixed by the regulations.

6. There shall be recourse to the Council of State in every case of abuse on the part of . . . ecclesiastical persons.

Cases of abuse are usurpation of power, violation of laws and regulations of the Republic, infraction of rules sanctioned by the canons received in France, attack upon the liberties, privileges, and customs of the Gallican church, and every undertaking or any proceeding which . . . can compromise the honor of the citizens, disturb . . . their consciences, or degenerate into oppression or injury against them or into public scandal. . . .

David L. Dowd, *Source Problems in World Civilizations: Napoléon, Was He the Heir of the Revolution?* Chicago: Holt, Rinehart and Winston, 1957, p. 48.

DOCUMENT 7: THE IMPERIAL CATECHISM

Napoléon was determined to associate his rule with the will of God. Toward that end he celebrated his birthday on August 15, the Feast of Assumption, which he designated as St. Napoléon Day. The Imperial Catechism, which he dictated to the French clergy, lays out the duties of Christians toward Napoléon and explains why the French people owe him loyalty and respect.

QUESTION: What are the duties of Christians in regard to the prince who governs them, and what are, in particular, our duties toward Napoléon I, our Emperor?

ANSWER: Christians owe the prince who governs them and we owe in particular to Napoléon I, our Emperor, love, respect, obedience, fidelity, military service, and the tributes laid for the preservation and defense of the Empire and of his throne; we also owe him fervent prayers for his safety and for the spiritual and temporal prosperity of the state.

QUESTION: Why do we owe all of these duties to our Emperor?

ANSWER: It is, first of all, because God who creates empires and distributes them according to His will, in endowing our Emperor with gifts, both in peace and in war, has established him as our sovereign, has given him the ministry of His power and of His image on earth.

QUESTION: What should one think of those who fail in their duty toward our Emperor?

ANSWER: According to the Apostle Saint Paul, they would be resisting the order established by God Himself and would be deserving of eternal damnation.

David L. Dowd, *Source Problems in World Civilizations: Napoléon, Was He the Heir of the Revolution?* Chicago: Holt, Rinehart and Winston, 1957, p. 53.

DOCUMENT 8: THE TEACHING CORPS

The following excerpt from February 16, 1805, describes the basic philosophy of the educational system that Napoléon established throughout France. Here he describes how a dedicated group of teachers would be held in high esteem by the public because the very stability of society rested in their hands. He also makes it clear that education was not for the sake of gaining more knowledge, but to train children how to be loyal French citizens.

At present, the teaching personnel consists of Principals, Proctors, and Professors. A teachers' corporation could be created if all the Principals, Proctors, and Professors of the Empire would be put under one or more head officials, just as the Jesuits were subordinate to a General, to Provincials, etc.; and if in order to be a Principal or Proctor it were required to have been a Professor first; if in order to teach in the upper grades, Professors first would have to teach in lower ones; and if, in fact, there existed in the teaching profession a regular system of promotion which would stimulate competition, so that, every stage in his life, a teacher not only had something to live on but also something to look forward to. A man who has devoted his life to teaching ought not to marry before he has passed through several stages of his career. Marriage ought to be for him, as for everyone else, a goal always before his eyes but that he can reach only after he has secured his place in society and financial independence by obtaining a position sufficiently remunerative to allow him to live as a head of a family without giving up his chosen career. Thus the teaching profession would be subject to the same conditions as the other civil service careers.

This [teachers'] organization would have its own *esprit de corps*. Its most distinguished members would be taken under the Emperor's protection and his patronage would raise them to a higher position in public esteem than that which the priests enjoyed in the times when priesthood was regarded as a kind of nobility. Everyone knew how important the Jesuits were; the importance of the corporation of teachers would be quickly realized if the public saw a talented man, after receiving his education at a *lycée*, called to teach in his turn, promoted from grade to grade, and, before the end of his career, take his place in first rank of state officials.

Of all political questions this one deserves perhaps the most attention. There will be no stability in the state until there is a teaching body based on established principles. So long as children are not taught whether they must be Republicans or Monarchists, Catholics or freethinkers, etc., the state will not constitute a nation but will rest on vague and shifting foundations, constantly exposed to change and disorder.

David L. Dowd, *Source Problems in World Civilizations: Napoléon, Was He the Heir of the Revolution?* Chicago: Holt, Rinehart and Winston, 1957, pp. 52–53.

DOCUMENT 9: EDUCATION FOR WOMEN

Upon Napoléon's restructuring of French schools, he ordered that all students be taught the same subjects in the same manner. However, this uniformity in instruction did not include girls. Although Napoléon agreed that girls should have an education, if only to keep them from being grossly ignorant or superstitious, he decreed that their education should concentrate on subjects that would make them better homemakers—such as religion, sewing, and cooking.

What should be taught the young ladies who will be brought up at Ecouen [a state school for girls]? First of all, religion in all its severity. In this respect you must be uncompromising. Religion is an important business in a public institution for young ladies. It is, no matter what has been said, the strongest safeguard for mothers and husbands. You must form believers, not reasoners. The weakness of women's brains, the mobility of their ideas, their destination in the social order, the necessity of constant and perpetual resignation and of a kind of indulgent and facile charitableness—all this can be obtained [sic!] only through religion, a charitable and gentle religion. . . .

Second, the pupils must be taught arithmetic, writing, and the rudiments of their language, so that they learn to spell correctly. They should be taught a little geography and history, but absolutely no Latin or foreign languages. The oldest ones may be taught a little botany and may be given a superficial course of physics or natural history, and at that there may be disadvantageous results. In physics, the teachers should limit themselves to the minimum needed to prevent gross ignorance and stupid superstition, and keep strictly to facts, without reasonings that bear directly or indirectly on first causes.

You will study the question whether it is convenient to give those who have reached a certain grade an allowance for their clothes. They might get used to economy, calculate the value of things, and make their own budgets.

In general, however, they should be kept busy, for three quarters of the year, at manual tasks. They should know how to knit stockings, make shirts, embroider, in a word, all sorts of feminine handiwork. . . .

I do not know if there is a possibility of teaching them a little medicine and pharmacy—at least, the kind of medicine a sicknurse ought to know. It would also be good if they had some acquaintance with that part of the kitchen that is called the pantry. I should like a young girl, when she leaves Ecouen to take her place at the head of a small household, to be able to make her own dresses, to mend her husband's clothes, to make her children's layettes . . . to nurse her husband and children when they are ill. . . .

I dare not prescribe, as I did at Fontainebleau [a military school for boys], that the pupils should learn cookery. I would have too many people against me. But the girls could be told to prepare their own desserts and whatever else may be given them either for their afternoon snack or their holidays. I dispense them from cooking, but not from making their own bread. The advantage of this is that they acquire practice in everything they may be called upon to do and that their time is naturally employed in practical and useful things.

Their rooms should be furnished by the work of their own hands. They should make their own underclothes, stockings, dresses, caps. All this is extremely important, in my opinion. I want these young girls to turn into useful women, convinced as I am that thus they will be agreeable women. I do not want to try to make agreeable women out of them, because they would merely turn into coquettes. Women who make their own dresses know how to dress tastefully.

Dancing is necessary to the health of the pupils, but it should be a jolly sort of dancing and none of your opera ballets. I shall also grant them music lessons, but vocal music only.

J. Christopher Herold, ed., *The Mind of Napoléon: A Selection from His Written and Spoken Words*, trans. J. Christopher Herold. New York: Columbia University Press, 1955, pp. 17–19.

DOCUMENT 10: THE ENGLISH SPIRIT

Though England proved to be Napoléon's greatest enemy, from the distance of his exile in St. Helena he offered the following kinder and gentler assessment of his former foes. In it he suggests that England's major strength rests on its foundation of commerce, and he cautions the English against changing.

You were greatly offended with me for having called you a nation of shopkeepers. Had I meant by this that you were a nation of cowards, you would have had reason to be displeased, even though it were ridiculous and contrary to historical facts; but no such thing was ever intended. I meant that you were a nation of merchants, and that all your great riches and your grand resources arose from commerce, which is true. What else constitutes the riches of England? It is not extent of territory or a numerous population. It is not mines of gold, silver, or diamonds. Moreover, no man of sense ought to be ashamed of being called a shopkeeper. But your prince and your ministers appear to wish to change altogether the *esprit* of the English and to make you into a different nation; to make you ashamed of your shops and your trade, which have made you what you are, and to sigh after nobility, titles, and decorations. . . . Stick to your ships, your commerce, and your countinghouses, and leave ribbons, decorations, and cavalry uniforms to the Continent, and you will prosper.

J. Christopher Herold, ed., *The Mind of Napoléon: A Selection from His Written and Spoken Words*, trans. J. Christopher Herold. New York: Columbia University Press, 1955, pp. 193–194.

Chronology

1769

Napoléon Bonaparte is born on August 15 in Corsica; the French force President Pasquale Paoli from Corsica, and he flees to England; England decides to retain tea taxes on American colonies; British governor dissolves Virginia Assembly for its resolutions against British taxes and other policies.

1776

British hang Nathan Hale for espionage; Thomas Paine publishes *Common Sense,* urging the end of America's union with Britain; the American colonies declare independence from Britain.

1779

Napoléon attends the military academy at Brienne in Champagne, France; Spain declares war on Britain; the French fail to recapture Savannah, Georgia.

1784

Napoléon enters the Royal Military School in Paris; Thomas Jefferson publishes *Notes on Virginia;* Benjamin Franklin invents bifocal eyeglasses; first school for the blind starts in Paris.

1785

Napoléon graduates and is commissioned as a lieutenant; Jefferson becomes minister to France; John Adams becomes minister to Great Britain.

1786–1788

Napoléon is on leave in Corsica.

1788

Napoléon enters artillery school in Auxonne; the U.S. Constitution is ratified.

1788–1789

Napoléon joins his regiment at Auxonne.

1789

The French Revolution begins; George Washington is chosen as first president of the United States.

1791

Napoléon joins the volunteer Corsican National Guard; Louis XVI accepts the new monarchial constitution, making him a mere figurehead; the Bill of Rights is ratified in the United States.

1792

Napoléon is promoted to lieutenant in Corsican National Guard and is soon promoted to captain; France declares war on Austria and Prussia; Austria and Prussia form the First Coalition against France; Louis XVI is deposed; the National Convention meets and abolishes the monarchy; the French Republic is inaugurated on September 21.

1793

France declares war on Britain and Holland, then on Spain; Corsican patriots revolt against France; the Bonaparte family travels to France for refuge; France recaptures Toulon from the British and royalists; Napoléon's role in the battle results in his promotion to brigadier general; France begins compulsory education from the age of six.

1794

Napoléon becomes artillery commander to the French army in Italy; Maximilien de Robespierre and the Jacobin government fall; Napoléon is arrested as part of the previous regime, then released and restored to rank.

1795

Napoléon puts down a royalist revolt in Paris, resulting in his promotion to major general in the Army of the Interior; France annexes Belgium and Luxembourg; National Convention ratifies a new constitution that establishes the Directory, made up of five members.

1796

Napoléon is appointed commander of the French army of Italy; marries Joséphine de Beauharnais; starts his first Italian campaign; forces the king of Sardinia to accept an armistice; makes his triumphant entry into Milan.

1797

Napoléon defeats the Austrians at Mantau in modern-day northern Italy; negotiates the Treaty of Tolentino with the papacy; under Napoléon's strong influence, the Peace of Leoben ends the first Italian campaign; a coup d'état eliminates the royalists; the Directory gives Napoléon a triumphant reception.

1798

The start of Napoléon's Egyptian campaign; the Second Coalition (Britain, Austria, Russia, Naples, and Turkey) forms against France; French law establishes conscription in French army; the U.S. Congress cancels all treaties with France and orders the U.S. Navy to capture all French ships.

1799

Napoléon leaves Egypt and returns to Paris; a coup d'état of 18th to 19th Brumaire ends the rule of the Directory, and, as a result, Napoléon is appointed First Consul; a new constitution is enacted.

1800

The start of Napoléon's second Italian campaign; Napoléon's life is threatened with a bomb plot; the Bank of France is founded; émigrés receive amnesty.

1801

Pope Pius VII signs the Concordat; the French army in Egypt surrenders to the British; the United Kingdom of Great Britain is established under one monarch and one parliament; the U.S. House of Representatives chooses Thomas Jefferson as president.

1802

Napoléon becomes president of the Republic of Italy; the Constitution of the Year X proclaims Napoléon first consul for life; the Treaty of Amiens is negotiated with Britain; Napoléon officially publishes the Concordat (with the Organic Articles); education law establishes lycées.

1803

Currency is reformed; the Treaty of Amiens is broken and war is renewed with Britain; France sells Louisiana to the United States.

1804

The Senate proclaims Napoléon hereditary emperor; Napoléon crowns himself emperor of France in Notre Dame Cathedral in Paris; a conspiracy against Napoléon is discovered and the plotters are arrested; the Civil Code is enacted; Spain is at war with Britain.

1805

Britain, Russia, and Austria form the Third Coalition against France; the French army invades Germany, resulting in the dissolution of the German Empire; creation of the Kingdom of Italy, with Napoléon being crowned king of Italy; Lord Horatio Nelson defeats the French at Trafalgar.

1806

Brother Joseph Bonaparte is crowned the king of Naples; brother Louis Bonaparte is crowned the king of Holland; the *Imperial Catechism* is published; the Fourth Coalition (Britain, Prussia, Russia, and some smaller states) forms against France; the Holy Roman Empire dissolves; the Berlin decree establishes the continental blockade against Britain; French troops enter Warsaw.

1807

Treaty of Tilsit with Russia and Prussia; establishment of the Kingdom of Westphalia and Grand Duchy of Warsaw; Napoléon abolishes the Tribunate; Russia declares war on Britain; Napoléon negotiates a secret treaty with Spain for the division of Portugal; the Decree of Milan intensifies the continental blockade against Britain.

1808

The French army occupies the Papal States; Napoléon appoints his brother-in-law Joachim Murat as lieutenant general in Spain; Murat suppresses Spanish rioters in bloody massacres; Joseph Bonaparte is crowned the king of Spain; Murat transfers to Naples; Napoléon assumes personal command of French army in Spain.

1809

The Fifth Coalition (Britain, Austria, and Spanish insurgents) forms against France, but Russia remains neutral; France annexes Papal States; Napoléon and Joséphine divorce; Pope Pius VII excommunicates Napoléon; Pius VII is arrested; Treaty of Schönbrunn with Austria.

1810

Rome, Holland, parts of Hanover, and the Grand Duchy of Oldenburg are annexed to the French Empire; Napoléon marries Marie-Louise of Austria.

1811

Birth of Napoléon's son, Napoléon II ("the King of Rome"); Napoléon holds Church Council of Paris, consisting of French and Italian bishops.

1812

The Sixth Coalition (Russia and Sweden, with British support) forms against France; Napoléon begins military campaign against Russia; he enters Moscow but retreats after failing to conquer it and returns to Paris, his army decimated.

1813

Pope Pius VII signs the Concordat of Fontainbleau (under pressure from Napoléon) and then repudiates it; Prussia and Austria declare war on France; Napoléon assumes command of the army and conquers Saxony; Arthur Wellesley, duke of Wellington, and his army force Joseph to flee Spain; Austria defeats Napoléon at Battle of Leipzig; Allies begin their invasion of France.

1814

Paris falls to the Allies; the French Senate strips Napoléon of the throne; Pope Pius VII is freed and returns to Italy; Napoléon abdicates; French borders are returned to where they were in 1792; Louis XVIII is restored to the throne; Napoléon is exiled to the island of Elba; unrest grows in France against the reactionary policies of the restored regime.

1815

Britain, Austria, and France form an alliance against Russia and Prussia; Napoléon escapes Elba and returns triumphantly to France; the Allies in Vienna outlaw Napoléon; Napoléon leaves Paris to take charge of the army; Wellington defeats Napoléon at Waterloo; Napoléon abdicates, surrenders to British, and is exiled to St. Helena; Louis XVIII returns to Paris.

1821

Napoléon dies on May 5.

1823

Publication of *Memoria I* by Emmanuel Las Cases, who stayed with Napoléon on St. Helena.

1840

Napoléon's remains are returned to Paris.

FOR FURTHER RESEARCH

ABOUT NAPOLÉON BONAPARTE

George G. Andrews, *Napoléon in Review.* New York: Knopf, 1939.

Jean-Baptiste Barrès, *Memoirs of a Napoléonic Officer,* trans. Bernard Miall. New York: Dial, 1925.

Louis Bergeron, *France Under Napoléon,* trans. R.R. Palmer. Princeton, NJ: Princeton University Press, 1981.

Antonty Brett-Janies, *The Hundred Days: Napoléon's Last Campaign from Eye-Witness Accounts.* New York: St. Martin's, 1964.

Michael Broers, *Europe Under Napoléon.* London: Arnold, 1996.

Dorothy Carrington, *Napoléon and His Parents: On the Threshold of History.* London: Viking, 1988.

Andre Castelot, *Napoléon,* trans. Guy Daniels. New York: Harper & Row, 1968.

David G. Chandler, *The Campaigns of Napoléon.* New York: Macmillan, 1966.

———, *On the Napoléonic Wars: Collected Essays.* London: Greenhill Books, 1994.

Owen Connelly, *Blundering to Glory: Napoléon's Military Campaigns.* Wilmington, DE: Scholarly Resources, 1987.

Gregor Dallas, *The Final Act: The Roads to Waterloo.* New York: Henry Holt, 1996.

Joseph Delteil, *Once There Was a Man Napoléon,* trans. Lewis Galantiere. New York: Covici-Friede, 1930.

David L. Dowd, *Source Problems in World Civilizations: Napoléon, Was He the Heir of the Revolution?* Chicago: Holt, Rinehart and Winston, 1957.

Roger Dufraisse, *Napoléon,* trans. Steven Englund. New York: McGraw-Hill, 1992.

Trevor N. Dupuy, *The Battle of Austerlitz: Napoléon's Greatest Victory.* New York: Macmillan, 1968.

Geoffrey Ellis, *Napoléon.* London: Longman, 1997.

Paul Frcgosi, *Dreams of Empire: Napoléon and the First World War 1792–1815.* London: Hutchinson, 1989.

Peter Geyl, *Napoléon: For and Against,* trans. Olive Renier. New Haven, CT: Yale University Press, 1967.

E.E.Y. Hales, *The Emperor and the Pope: The Story of Napoléon and Pius VII.* Garden City, NY: Doubleday, 1961.

David Hamilton-Williams, *The Fall of Napoléon: The Final Betrayal.* New York: John Wiley and Sons, 1994.

Philip J. Haythornthwaite, et al., *Napoléon: The Final Verdict.* London: Arms and Armour, 1996.

Robert B. Holtman, *Napoléonic Propaganda.* Baton Rouge: Louisiana State University Press, 1961.

———, *The Napoléonic Revolution.* Baton Rouge: Louisiana State University Press, 1967.

Alistair Horne, *How Far from Austerlitz?: Napoléon 1805–1815.* New York: St. Martin's, 1996.

———, *Napoléon: Master of Europe 1805–1807.* London: Weidenfeld and Nicholson, 1979.

Ben R. Jones, *Napoléon: Man and Myth.* London: Hodder and Stoughton, 1977.

Georges Lefebvre, *Napoléon: From 18 Brumaire to Tilsit 1799–1807,* trans. Henry F. Stockold. New York: Columbia University Press, 1969.

———, *Napoléon: From Tilsit to Waterloo 1807–1815,* trans. J.E. Anderson. New York: Columbia University Press, 1969.

John E. Lewis, ed., *The Mammoth Book of Eye-witness History.* New York: Carroll & Graf, 1998.

Martyn Lyons, *Napoléon Bonaparte and the Legacy of the French Revolution.* New York: St. Martin's, 1994.

Philip Mansel, *The Eagle in Splendour: Napoléon I and His Court.* London: George Philip, 1987.

F.M.H. Markham, *Napoléon and the Awakening of Europe.* London: English Universities Press, 1961.

Anthony Masters, *Napoléon.* New York: McGraw-Hill, 1981.

Frank McLynn, *Napoléon: A Biography.* London: Jonathan Cape, 1997.

Dmitri Merezhkovsky, *Napoléon the Man,* trans. Catherine Zvegintzov. New York: E.P. Dutton, 1928.

Ines Murat, *Napoléon and the American Dream,* trans. Frances Frenaye. Baton Rouge: Louisiana State University Press, 1981.

David H. Pinkney, ed., *Napoléon: Historical Enigma.* Lexington, MA: D.C. Heath, 1969.

Michael Polowetzky, *A Bond Never Broken: The Relationship Between Napoléon and the Authors of France.* London: Associated University Press, 1993.

Claire Elisabeth Jeanne Gravier De Vergennes Remusat, *Memoirs of the Empress Josephine.* New York: P.F. Collier & Son, 1879.

Gunther E. Rothenberg, *The Napoléonic Wars.* London: Cassell, 1999.

Jean Savant, *Napoléon in His Time.* London: Putnam, 1958.

Alan Schom, *Napoléon Bonaparte.* New York: HarperCollins, 1997.

Desmond Seward, *Napoléon and Hitler.* New York: Viking, 1989.

Stendhal, *A Life of Napoléon.* London: Rodale, 1956.

Jean Tulard, *Napoléon: The Myth of the Saviour.* London: Weidenfeld and Nicholson, 1984.

ABOUT NAPOLÉON'S TIMES

Geoffrey Brunn, *Europe and the French Imperium 1799–1814.* New York: Harper & Row, 1938.

Thomas Carlyle, *The French Revolution.* New York: Modern Library, 1901.

Will Durant and Ariel Durant, *The Age of Napoléon.* New York: Simon & Schuster, 1975.

J. Christopher Herold, *The Age of Napoléon.* New York: American Heritage, 1963.

Walter Markov, *Grand Empire: Virtue and Vice in the Napoléonic Era.* New York: Hippocrene Books, 1990.

Arnold Toynbee, *A Study of History.* New York: Oxford University Press, 1972.

BY NAPOLÉON BONAPARTE

Jean-Pierre Babelon and Suzanne D'huart, *Napoléon's Last Will and Testament,* trans. Alex de Jonge. New York: Paddington Press, 1977.

Napoléon Bonaparte, *Memoirs,* trans. Somerset De Chair. London: Soho, 1986.

——, *Napoléon on Napoléon,* trans. Somerset De Chair. London: Cassell, 1992.

J. Christopher Herold, ed., *The Mind of Napoléon: A Selection from His Written and Spoken Words,* trans. J. Christopher Herold. New York: Columbia University Press, 1955.

WEBSITES

Napoléon (www.napoleon.org) Museum, documents, and information on Napoléon.

Napoléon Bonaparte Internet Guide (www.iselinge.nl/ napoleon) Links, resources, historical and other information related to Napoléon and Napoléonic history.

Napoléonic Literature (www.napoleonic-literature. simplenet.com) Books and art in electronic format.

The Napoléon Series (www.historyserver.org/napoleon. series) Discussion forum, as well as sections on military, research, and reviews.

INDEX